VANCOUVER DEFENDED

A History of the
Men and Guns of the
Lower Mainland Defences,
1859-1949

by Peter N. Moogk
assisted by Major R.V. Stevenson

ANTONSON PUBLISHING LTD.

To all the former gunners and those others who shared their memories with us and, by doing so, made this book possible.

©PETER N. MOOGK, 1978

All rights reserved. No part of this book to be reproduced or transmitted in any form by any means without permission in writing from the publisher, except by a reviewer, who may quote brief passages in a review.

Antonson Publishing Ltd.
Editorial Office:
12165 — 97th Avenue
Surrey
British Columbia

ISBN 0-919900-26-7

Photographs by the author unless otherwise credited

Layout by Frebo Studio Limited

Printed in Canada by Hemlock Printers Ltd.

Moogk, Peter N., 1943 -
Vancouver defended

ISBN 0-919900-26-7

1. British Columbia - Militia. 2. Canada - Coast defences. 3. Firearms - History. I. Title.
FC3845.L69M65   971.11'33   C77-002155-7
F1089

VANCOUVER DEFENDED

Contents

Foreword - Reg H. Roy 7

Introduction - Peter N. Moogk 8

Chapter 1. Inauspicious Beginnings at New Westminster 12

Chapter 2. Sham Battles at Vancouver, 1859-1899 22

Chapter 3. Cruisers Loose in the Pacific 31

Chapter 4. Marking Time Between the Wars 54

Chapter 5. Take Post! 61

Chapter 6. Going Yorkey: Yorke Island, 1939-1945 85

Chapter 7. Hurry Up and Wait 94

Chapter 8. Recessional 104

Appendix: A Chronological List of Artillery Units, 1866-1949 114

Bibliography 116

Chapter Notes 118

Index 124

Foreword

British Columbia has been an extremely fortunate province. It has never experienced the shock of rebellion nor the scars of war. There are no battlefield memorials within its boundaries and only once were a few enemy shells fired against its shores. It has had a peaceful existence far from the powder-kegs of Europe and the Pacific rim of Asia.

Despite the measure of safety which geographic remoteness has provided, British Columbia has frequently feared the onslaught of war. The Crimean War resulted in the first permanent construction at the naval station at Esquimalt. Some two decades later, the threat of another Anglo-Russian war brought about the erection of the first coastal artillery batteries to defend the naval base and the provincial capital. The completion of the Canadian Pacific Railway and the subsequent growth of Vancouver made the mainland an increasingly important area in the overall scheme of national and imperial defence. During the Great War of 1914-1918 and especially the Second World War, Canada sent thousands of men and spent millions of dollars to ensure that her citizens on the Pacific Coast would be protected against any enemy raid by sea, land or air.

This book covers a period of approximately 100 years and focusses its attention on the role played by artillerymen defending Vancouver and its environs. It is a story of struggle, of constant attempts by a few far-sighted men to have the federal government provide the basic measures for defence during decades when the warning bugles of approaching conflict seemed very distant indeed. It is a story of patriotism and self-sacrifice on the part of gunners of all ranks in the militia who tried to maintain some semblance of military capability in the face of government indifference. It is a story which needed to be told, for in this new age we shall no longer have the time, as our forefathers did, to equip and train ourselves for war behind the "wooden walls of England" or the once vast distance between British Columbia and the rest of the world.

Reginald H. Roy, C.D., Ph.D.,
Professor of Military & Strategic Studies,
University of Victoria.

Introduction

This book grew out of a chance meeting and concern for an historic site. In the spring of 1974 I met Major Vic Stevenson, historian of the 15th Field Artillery Regiment, in connection with a small display on the Royal Canadian Artillery put on in the History and Economics Reading Room of the University of British Columbia. It was something that I had put together, as a member of the History Department at U.B.C., to mark the thirtieth anniversary of the campaign to liberate northwestern Europe from the Nazis. Our conversation came round to the Point Grey gun battery, which was located on the university campus, and Vic sketched out the details of this Second World War installation. This was a revelation to me for, though as an adolescent in Holland I had played among the concrete remains of Hitler's Festung Europa and had recognized the structures on the point as bunkers of some sort, their true nature was a mystery.

In the summer of that year the centre section of the battery was dynamited and levelled to make way for the new Museum of Anthropology. The smaller, flanking gun emplacements seemed also to be destined for oblivion for the architect's plans would have buried them in the university's second Oriental garden. It was rather ironic that the Asian menace that the battery was built to repel had finally triumphed. The new museum was certainly a desirable asset to the city. Yet it puzzled me that military history of Point Grey was not only being ignored, it was also being completely buried. Historians are supposed to have scruples about revising the past to please the present and I felt obliged to raise the question "should a part of the Point Grey battery be preserved (as an historic site)?" From December 1974 onward this question was put to various groups and the general public. The answer, I am happy to say, was affirmative.

I became the champion of historical preservation by default; it was not a natural role for a specialist in the social history of early French Canada. Apart from a few students, there was little interest on the U.B.C. campus in this site; most of the people who worked there did not know that the battery had ever existed. There was also a prejudice to be overcome, one that associated an interest in military history with bloodlust and militarism. In short, it appeared that if I did not act nobody else would and the site would disappear from view.

Before appealing for the conservation of at least one gun emplacement, I had to educate myself on the history of the Vancouver defences. There was no publication on that subject and so the story had to be pieced together from a variety of sources. My two principal instructors were Vic Stevenson and Captain Jack Rippengale of Fort Rodd Hill Historic Park. Brigadier R.T. DuMoulin also answered an infinity of questions on this or that point. My research into the period before 1939 was facilitated by the information gathered at the beginning of this century by Lieut. Col. F.A. Robertson of Victoria and Major James Skitt Matthews, the founder of the Vancouver City Archives. Without their preliminary work, research into the history of the local militia would have been a monumental task. One would have also contracted a fatal case of microfilm reader's eyes. In the light of my experience at U.B.C., it was amusing to discover that the university campus owed its existence to a military reserve established in the nineteenth century; "militarism" did have benefits, after all! Armed with some knowledge of local history and a few illustrations, it was now possible to discuss the merits of the Point Grey site.

The appeal to the public began with a short article in the Winter 1974 issue of the **U.B.C. Alumni Chronicle.** The editor, Susan Jamieson McLarnon, listened to me with an infectious enthusiasm and the article was written post haste to make that issue's deadline. Susan's response was the harbinger of things to come, for popular interest in the history of the Vancouver defences seemed insatiable. After more articles, several radio programmes and two television shows, the requests for further information kept pouring in. In addition to the notes of appreciation, there were telephone calls and letters containing personal recollections of the war years. One of the mishaps of the Second World War was the shelling of a freighter in English Bay on the anniversary of the Battle of the Plains of Abraham. What a shock it was to receive a call from the commander of the guilty battery, a latter-day Wolfe, who was assumed to be on the other side of eternity. All of this new information was added to a growing research file and some of the new informants are quoted in the text. Drawing attention to what had been a neglected aspect of local history was a very satisfying experience and it led, with the expressed support of others, to the preservation of the No. 1 Gun emplacement on Point Grey.

Before I escaped to Cape Breton in September 1975 for a sabbatical year, discussions had begun with the publisher, Rick Antonson, about producing a more detailed and enduring account of the artillery on the Lower Mainland of British Columbia. The problems of gathering material were underestimated and Rick demonstrated those virtues of a good publisher: patience and firmness. Vic Stevenson sped things up by offering, not only his expert criticism, but also to write chapters 4 and 6. No one is better qualified than Vic to write the early history of his regiment or the story of Yorke Island, his not-so-secret passion. A number of photographs from his collection and that of the 15th Field Artillery Regiment were used as illustrations. He has been a marvellous co-author. A word of thanks is due as well to Reg. H. Roy of the University of Victoria, B.C.'s premier military historian, who gave the entire manuscript a careful "once-over" and drew our attention to a number of errors and omissions. Alan Woodland of the New Westminster Public Library performed the same service on chapter one.

This illustrated history of the artillery on the Lower Mainland is meant to be an accurate and entertaining account of the past. In it I have tried to evoke the spirit of the times and to reconstruct the lives of the gunners. Whenever possible, the participants and the documents have been allowed to speak for themselves. Paraphrasing distorts the original source and the uncritical repetition of other secondary works leads to additional errors of fact. Having observed the blunders of earlier works, we have no illusions about our own effort being perfect and definitive. If readers find it a reliable and readable history, we shall be content.

For an historian whose customary fare is the lives of people long dead and removed from the present by centuries, the interviewing of informants has been a novel and exciting experience. Public records will always preserve names and dates but it is the memories of those who were present that give life to the story. Many of the episodes that they recalled were absent from the official record or only received brief and uninformative mention. The informants also remembered small things which, though not important in themselves, threw light on their situation and their feelings at the time. Veterans of the Second World War were particularly numerous and cooperative and their massive contribution is reflected in the proportions of the book. Some are quoted and more are acknowledged as sources in the footnotes. I regret that I could not thank everyone by name for having supplied a detail or an anecdote or for simply confirming facts.

Though Vic and I have been associated with the Canadian Army, we have attempted to avoid writing a partisan account. There is a tendency in regimental histories to swamp the reader with facts and to portray one's officers as far-sighted and persevering and the other ranks as consistently keen and brave. This book is a portrait "warts and all," to use Oliver Cromwell's expression. There are things in the narrative that are admirable and there are others that are not. To do otherwise would not have been to write history. Since we learn from our mistakes, a more favourable and selective account would not have been instructive. "The lessons of history" is an abused phrase and yet this history does lead to certain conclusions. To judge from the ninety years studied, these lessons were either unrecognized or ignored.

The principal observation applies to successive Canadian governments. Every military crisis has found us ill-prepared to meet the external challenge. By chance, our makeshift and threadbare defences have not been seriously tested. Between crises Canada has limped along with a poorly-equipped army that, when it was given a clearly-defined role, usually lacked the means to fulfil it. This history shows that, more often than not, the militia was armed with obsolete and inadequate equipment and that this undermined morale. Armaments are expensive and it is all too easy for the national government in peacetime to cut back on defence rather than in some area where the effects of retrenchment would be immediately felt by a large segment of society. In Canada the result has been a paper army whose deficiencies in equipment had to be made good by our allies in emergencies. To anyone interested in the political independence of Canada or even the efficient expenditure of public money, this drifting policy makes little sense. By all appearances, however, it is a grand Canadian tradition.

In the armed forces a Canadian military tradition was a long time in coming and it is still not very strong. When I undertook research for this book, I hoped to find out how the militia fitted into the local community, what sort of persons joined the reserve army and why they did so. The beginning of an answer to those questions has been sketched out in this book. Until very recently, the militia served as a fraternal association for men, including the most influential members of Vancouver society. Before the Second World War the appeal of part-time soldiering was strongest for those of British ancestry. This reflected the traditions of the Canadian army. Our armed forces, at their inception, modelled themselves on those of Great Britain. Before 1920, when the bonds of politics and affection between the two countries were so strong, this was a natural thing to do; Britain was the mother country of the young Dominion. The Canadian army remained self-consciously British for another quarter century and this association with one cultural group weakened the appeal of the militia for those of a different ethnic background. The nominal rolls are cited as evidence of this pattern. There were exceptions such as Napoleon LaBranche of Quebec who joined Vancouver's first militia company and took a hand in the formation of the second one. Presently the Canadian armed forces more closely reflect the cultural and racial makeup of our country, which is good, though the old imitative tendency persists. This time the model is provided by the United States rather than Great Britain.

This book shows in dramatic ways how officers can affect the morale of their subordinates for good or ill. By personality alone Captain George Pittendrigh kept the New Westminster Battery going in the 1880's despite the unit's decrepit guns and baggy uniforms. When inexperienced and inept officers were appointed to the battery in 1894 the gunners mutinied. These are examples of the best and the worst that a leader can do in motivating subordinates. It was astonishing to observe what a lasting impression was made by officers who were capable and considerate or, conversely, callous and sarcastic. If the feelings aroused by these qualities can survive after thirty-five years, one can easily imagine their effect during the last world war. The visible concern of an officer or anyone in authority for the welfare and comfort of those under that person's command has won enduring trust and loyalty.

These observations show that even a local history can contain themes of universal significance. Such points are really incidental to our story. The book was not written as a sermon; it is a recollection of a bygone era that began in 1859 and ended in 1949. In 1859 the first reserves were established for the defence of Burrard Inlet and 1949 saw the closure of the last coast artillery installation on the Lower Mainland, the Point Grey Battery. The intervening ninety years belonged to an age when seaborne attack was most feared and against which land-based guns were reckoned the best defence. Flying bombers and guided missles drew the curtain on that age. Through this book and its pictures the reader is invited to return to that epoch when, for most people, "atom" meant the smallest particle of matter rather than greatest destructive force imaginable.

Peter N. Moogk

CHAPTER 1

Inauspicious Beginnings at New Westminster

European settlement on British North America's Pacific coast was largely confined to Vancouver Island until 1856. In that year large gold deposits were discovered in the sandbars of the Fraser and Thompson Rivers. Before then the mainland north of the United States had been a wild hinterland sprinkled with Amerindian villages and Hudson's Bay Company posts. Word of the gold strike brought a flood of rootless adventurers north from the Oregon Territory, California and abroad. This was an alien and disorderly horde, whose principal amusements were gambling, drunkeness and prostitution. Its presence was a challenge to British authority, represented by the infant administration at Fort Victoria on the island. The administration's ideal was a God-fearing, law-abiding, and loyal British community. To forestall the violence and vigilante "justice" experienced in the California gold rush, the island government extended its jurisdiction to the mining population. The response of the imperial government in London was to create an entirely separate colony on the mainland and to call it "British Columbia." The new administration was inaugurated in November 1858 when James Douglas took his oath as governor of the colonies of British Columbia and Vancouver Island. Without a proper capital or a civil service, the new colony existed in law but not in fact.

Governor Douglas favoured Fort Langley, a post on the Fraser River, as the future capital of British Columbia. In 1859 he was persuaded to accept another location, just fifteen miles from the river's mouth and on an uncleared slope. The town was also on the north shore of the Fraser and less vulnerable to a sudden American incursion. To remind the unruly miners that political authority came from Queen Victoria and her parliament at Westminster, the site was named "New Westminster." It had briefly been known as Queensborough. The man who had induced Douglas to accept the location and who planned the future administrative centre was Colonel Richard Clement Moody. Col. Moody was part of the 165 man Columbia Detachment of the British army's Royal Engineers. These soldiers were sent to the mainland colony to serve as a ready-made civil service and police force. The sappers surveyed townsites, built roads and bridges, erected churches and public buildings, and printed government decrees as well as postage stamps. They

12

were an example of the government enterprise that has been a central feature of Canadian life and their work converted British Columbia from a legal fiction to a living reality. By 1863 a civilian administration was ready to assume these public services and the Columbia Detachment of the Royal Engineers was disbanded. Their contribution was not at an end; most of the soldiers chose to remain in North America and, as individuals, they continued to aid in the development of the colonies.

The disbanding of the Columbia Detachment deprived the mainland colony of that one service which only disciplined and trained soldiers could provide: an armed defence force. In November 1863 a committee at New Westminster in a letter to Sir James Douglas proposed the formation of a volunteer or militia rifle company. The suggestion was forwarded to the Colonial Secretary's Office in Britain and there it was approved. Arms and equipment were promised once the unit's officers had been elected. With this promise, the New Westminster Volunteer Rifles, comprising 70 to 80 men, came into being.

The volunteer infantry company seemed adequate for the defence of the colony until 1866. The new threat, strangely enough, originated in Ireland which was still under British rule. At Dublin, in the very year that British Columbia was named, the supporters of Irish independence formed the Fenian Brotherhood. Their model was the **fiann**, the bodyguard of the ancient Irish kings. Irish immigrants carried the cause across the Atlantic Ocean to North America. Many learned the bloody trade of soldiering in the United States' Civil War and with that war's end in 1865 they were recruited by the Fenians. A seaborne landing in Ireland was too hazardous, yet British North America lay open to overland invasion. An attack against the sprawling and poorly-defended North American colonies would be a blow against Great Britain and the Irish republicans, if victorious, might be able to use them to bargain for Ireland's freedom. In the spring of 1866 Fenian raids were made against New Brunswick and the future provinces of Quebec and Ontario. The small Irish-American armies left destruction and panic in their wake before they retired to the United States. No part of British North America was immune: Fenian agents entered the Red River colony (Manitoba) and an eccentric named George Francis Train called on Fenians in San Francisco to conquer British Columbia. Train planned to build a wooden bridge across Juan de Fuca Straight to facilitate the conquest of Vancouver Island. Fortunately, this scheme and Train's prediction that he would be the president of the United States never came to pass.

The alarm created in 1866 by the Fenian attacks in Eastern Canada was mirrored in an editorial in the **British Columbian** titled "Fenianism -- Our Situation." "Whatever sympathy we may have with the sufferings of unhappy Ireland," wrote the editor, "there is no mistaking our duty in the present emergency. While we are calling upon the Government to extend to us a fair share of the protection of the fleet, let us prove ourselves worthy of that protection by organizing for defence; let us emulate those noble fellows who fought so gallantly at the battle of Ridgeway (against the Fenian invaders) and, if we cannot hope to conquer, let us at least sell our lives dearly and die like Britons -- British Columbia expects that every man will do his duty."[1] The same issue of June 16th, 1866 reported the meeting of the New Westminster municipal council at which resolutions were presented to form a committee to press the government "for measures of defence" and to create a new corps to support the existing rifle company. The second infantry unit, The Home Guards, would include males above the age of 18 who were not qualified for the older corps. The Guards lasted until about 1871. It was noted that the resolution for their creation "gave rise to considerable discussion in the course of which an Artillery Corps was spoken of and an amendment offered."[2]

It is apparent from an accompanying report in the **British Columbian** that arrangements for an artillery unit were already being made. The initiator was a former gunner, Captain G.W. Holmes, who had been Governor Frederick Seymour's private secretary. According to the newspaper, "Captain Holmes has been so fortunate as to secure a number of ex-Royal Engineers, who have been more or less training in Artillery tactics, and the guns, etc., are expected to arrive immediately. There can be no doubt that an Artillery Company would be of great advantage in case of an attack."[3] A subsequent issue described the public meeting on defence measures held at New Westminster on the evening of Saturday, June 16th. "After the work of organizing the Home Guards was got through," stated the **British Columbian,** "measures were taken for organizing the Artillery Company, when Captain Holmes, R.A., was unanimously chosen Captain of the Company, after which they adopted the name of "Seymour Artillery Company" (in honour of the governor). On Monday they (the two new units) received their arms and marched through the city in excellent style. The Seymour Artillery Company has the advantage of being mainly composed of ex-Royal Engineers, and is now something over 40 strong...This city can now boast of three Volunteer Military Companies,...numbering in all 180 men. There are doubtless many others who will yet join, but even this is by no means a bad beginning for New Westminster, and affords tolerably conclusive evidence that: should the Fenians venture upon our shores they will not, at least, be permitted to take peaceable possession."[4]

On Monday, July 16th, the "Artillery Volunteer Corps" met in the Legislative Council Hall under the chairmanship of Captain Holmes and, in successive ballots, voted on the admission of new recruits. They then elected their junior and non-commissioned officers. A total of ten posts were thus filled. Military units are generally associated with subordination and these democratic proceedings might seem odd to the modern reader. It was, in fact, the most practical means of setting up a new hierarchy and the practice was sanctioned by the custom of the times. Officers voted on the admission of others to their ranks and they could "Blackball" undesirables. The command structure of the Seymour Artillery Company in July 1866 was as follows, with the former Royal Engineers marked with an asterisk:[5]

Commanding Officer	- Captain G.W. Holmes
Senior Lieutenant and musketry instructor	- David McCullock
Second Lieutenant	- Henry P.P. Crease
Surgeon	- W.S. Black
Battery Sergeant-Major	- George Hand*
Sergeant	- John Murray*
Corporals	- Robert Cowan
	- John Linn*
Bombardier	- John Smith*
Acting Bombardier	- Lancelot Newton
Trumpeter	- A. Cummings (probably Allan Cummins*)

The unpublished records of the artillery company have been lost and it is not possible to identify all of its personnel. From this short list, it is evident that at the top the unit was not "mainly composed of ex-Royal Engineers." It is also noteworthy that the two gunners who were in the Columbia Detachment, Sgt. James Lindsay and Cpl. William Bowden, were not associated with the Seymour Artillery Company though they lived in the New Westminster District at the time.

The effusive reports of the **British Columbian** give the impression that the members of the artillery corps were properly uniformed and armed; it was not so. Their guns, rifles, shot, powder and accoutrements were sent out from England and did not reach Victoria until the following year. The man who, as officer commanding the Seymour Artillery Company, requested delivery of the equipment to New Westminster was none other than the junior lieutenant, Henry P. Pellew Crease. Crease was Attorney-General of British Columbia and, undoubtedly, a capable man. Yet his rapid ascent to command of the artillery company was a clue that all was not well with the mainland gunners. His men not only lacked guns; they were unpaid and were obliged to supply their own uniforms. Judging from Lieut. Crease's other requests for the use of various public buildings as a drill hall, it appears that the unit was homeless for some time. The company shared the Volunteer Rifles' drill shed for the greater part of its history. Crease must have been relieved in October 1867 when he acknowledged the delivery of the artillery pieces and munitions. The arms were brought to the Royal City by H.M.S. **Sparrowhawk,** a gun vessel stationed at Esquimalt. The artillery company had not received a full battery of four guns; it had been sent two brass, smooth-bore, muzzle-loading, 24 pounder howitzers on wheeled, field carriages. These guns, whose five foot barrels were cast in 1858 and 1859, were of an old design and rapid technical advances in gunnery soon made them outmoded. The two howitzers, despite this, remained the principal armament of the New Westminster battery until 1892 and, probably, until its demise.

The high hopes that had accompanied the creation of the artillery company were unjustified and the later history of the unit is a pathetic chronicle of sagging morale that was ultimately related to the guns. The unit's fate paralleled the misfortunes of New Westminster. When the gold rush petered out the mining population moved on and the number of white inhabitants in the mainland colony shrank. In its reduced state, British Columbia did not merit the expense of a separate administration and so, in 1866, the mainland was legally united with Vancouver Island to form the new colony of British Columbia. The government of the enlarged colony lingered at New Westminster for two years before being permanently transferred to Victoria. With the government's departure went the senior officials, including Henry Crease, who had given a social lustre to the officers of the local militia. When New Westminster ceased to be the capital in 1868, it fell on hard times that were to endure until the arrival of the railway in 1887. Even then the Royal City could not match the growth of that rival upstart on Burrard Inlet, the City of Vancouver.

On July 20th, 1871 British Columbia became a province of Canada; it was the beginning of a new regime for the militia on the Pacific coast. No longer would the volunteer units communicate directly with the War Office in Britain, as they had done in the old crown colonies. The part-time soldiers were now subject to the Canadian Department of the Militia. In 1872 Canada's Adjutant-General of Militia, Col. Patrick Robertson-Ross, made a personal inspection of the westernmost province and he recommended "the formation of two companies of riflemen in Victoria, and one at Nanaimo,...also the formation of one company of riflemen at New Westminster, another at Burrard's Inlet on the mainland and that the New Westminster Battery of Garrison Artillery be reorganised."[6]

The last recommendation was carried out and on July 10th, **1874 the gunners of New Westminster were incorporated into the Canadian militia as the Seymour Battery of Garrison Artillery.** Lieut. John F. Scott and Second Lieut. Ebenezer Brown were gazetted as officers of the battery. The unit was still the poor cousin of the militia infantry, whose drill shed, magazine and rifle range it shared. The continued poverty of the gunners was revealed by the 1875 report of the officer commanding the Canadian militia, Major-General Sir Edward Selby-Smyth. The report proposed that "the usual ammunition for practice be allowed the Seymour Artillery, the cost of which has heretofore been defrayed by the commanding officer."[7] This expense made command of the battery unattractive and when Lieut. Scott prepared to give up his post in 1876, before moving from the city, he had no successor. Indeed, the ranks of his command had thinned from 18 in 1875 to just 12 in 1876. The newly-instituted remuneration of fifty cents per soldier for every full day in training was small reward in a province where a man could earn four times that amount as an unskilled worker. The population was also very mobile and it was hard to secure a reliable body of men who would remain in the area. Moreover, equipment had been scattered throughout the community as former members of the artillery company kept what they had received. The Deputy Adjutant-General in the province, Lieut. Col. Charles Frederick Houghton, took stock of the situation in a private meeting with eight of the remaining gunners on December 7th, 1876. There he learned "that the corps had recently for various reasons become thoroughly disorganized." He therefore agreed "to recommend the disbandment or re-organization of the Seymour Artillery as the best and surest method of replacing it in a state of efficiency." Lieut. Scott's management of the equipment was not entirely at fault; the company had taken on recruits who lived well outside New Westminster and they could not serve as effective members of the battery. It was Col. Houghton's wish that, henceforth, recruiting be restricted to "residents within the city…and its immediate vicinity, who take considerable interest in the organization."[8]

Ineffective command, loss of equipment and unselective recruiting were all compounded by another cause for demoralization: the state of the battery's guns. In 1876 Lieut. Col. Houghton wrote that "Lieutenant Scott, commanding Seymour Artillery, reported to me that when recently removing one of the 24-pounder brass guns from the open platform to the drill shed for winter drill purposed, one of the wheels had broken down completely. On examination of the broken wheel, I found it to be thoroughly rotten. This was temporarily replaced by one taken off one of the limbers; but I find the entire carriage is scarcely any better than the wheel, and I consider it would be very unsafe to attempt to use the gun for practice in its present condition. The other carriage appears to be in somewhat better condition, however, and as the guns themselves are of little value except for the material in them, I would not recommend any money being spent in repairing them."[9] This suited the thrifty inclinations of the Dominion Government which did not provide funds for either the repair or replacement of these decrepit weapons.

Without new guns, even an experienced and energetic commander was hard put to breathe life into the moribund battery. The experience of George Pittendrigh, who commanded the New Westminster gunners for seven and a half years, was proof of this. Captain Pittendrigh, a fishery inspector and magistrate, assumed command in 1878 from the acting C.O., Sgt. J.R. Wiesenborn. Pittendrigh was all that one might wish of an officer: he was a Crimean War veteran who had served in the 3rd Regiment of Infantry and his zeal was evident in his willingness to accept a temporary demotion to the rank of lieutenant to achieve command of the artillery company. His ambition was to acquire a full battery of four new guns and to bring the unit up to its authorized strength of two officers and thirty other ranks.

World circumstances gave a brief assist to Captain Pittendrigh's efforts. Britain was determined to prop up the crumbling Turkish Empire and when Russian forces threatened to overwhelm the Turks a war between Britain and Russia seemed imminent. With bases on the Pacific Ocean, the Russian navy could menace the exposed shores of British Columbia. The province was all the more important to the Royal Navy because it was the sole British territory in the Eastern Pacific Ocean and a source of coal for steam-powered vessels. This consideration hastened the building of defences for Victoria and Esquimalt harbours and it made the Dominion government more responsive to the needs of the militia in the distant province. Twenty-five new uniforms were issued to the Seymour Battery, but like most army clothing it came in just two sizes: too large and too small. On his annual inspection, Lieut. Col. Houghton allowed that "some" of the uniforms "will be improved by alterations" and he seconded a request for five more outfits so that the unit could recruit up to its authorized strength of thirty men. Captain Pittendrigh had already raised the battery to two officers and twenty-one men by December 1878 and he was confident of enlisting more. Despite the ill-fitting uniforms and the inexperience of the new recruits, they acquitted themselves well "in a few simple company movements under Captain Pittendrigh, who proves himself an efficient instructor in drill." Houghton also watched them go through a firing exercise with one of the guns which "was fairly performed."[10] The gunners were keen enough to have bought their own spiked helmets to go with the new uniforms.

This enthusiasm could not be sustained without new guns and by 1879 attendance for training fell off and the drill of those on parade was half-hearted. Captain Pittendrigh bore some of the blame since, in his desire for more recruits, he had enlisted men living outside the city. This was contrary to Col. Houghton's wish. When the danger of a war with Russia had passed, the replacement of the battery's guns was again put off by the Department of the Militia. In 1880 the Deputy Adjutant-General reported with sympathy that "Captain Pittendrigh complains -- not without good cause -- that an artillery corps without guns is an anomaly most difficult to sustain; the men losing interest, and the public regarding them in the light of a useless piece of pageantry, of which the wearing of a uniform is the principal object."[11] One gun was utterly useless and the other venerable piece was handled with gentle caution lest it disintegrate too. As a rule, the men simply went through the motions of gun drill and then verbally recited the steps for loading and firing. One can imagine that the little band of militia gunners in their poorly-fitted uniforms and with their decaying field pieces was an obvious target for local wits.

As for pageantry, the Seymour Battery was a frequent participant in the public ceremonies of New Westminster and elsewhere. Since 1868 the local gunners had fired the royal salute on Queen Victoria's birthday, the 24th of May. The salute supplemented and then replaced the **feu de joie** of the New Westminster Volunteers' rifles. The artillery salute was traditionally fired at noon on Victoria Day from "the battery" opposite Albert Crescent. In 1870 the arrival of the queen's birthday at midnight was heralded with a single discharge and music by the down band. "After two guns were fired," reported the **Mainland Guardian** of May 28th, "the band played 'God Save the Queen' with splendid effect; the strains of this unequalled national hymn vibrating in the stillness of the night, produced a feeling of solemnity mixed with awe." After the customary royal salute at midday the battery's acting commander, Dr. Black, reappeared to masquerade as "Aunt Sally." In this curious ritual that was sometimes performed on May Day a white person was disguised as "an over-dressed klootchman" or an Indian woman in European dress and blanket with a clay pipe in her mouth. The onlookers then attempted to smash her pipe, which was frequently replaced.[12]

After confederation with Canada in 1871 Dominion Day became a public holiday. In the late nineteenth century it was not celebrated in British Columbia with the same enthusiasm as Victoria Day. British Columbians felt greater attachment for Britain than for the land beyond the mountains and they resented the delayed completion of the transcontinental railway, which was promised at the time of confederation. In the Royal City July 1st was passed in sports events, maritime excursions and an evening dance. From 1873 onward shiploads of holidaymakers from New Westminster, Victoria and Nanaimo converged on Burrard Inlet to share in the Dominion Day celebrations. This pattern continued after the completion of the railroads and the foundation of the city of Vancouver.

The deplorable condition of the Seymour Battery's guns imperilled the royal salute to Her Majesty. In the autumn of 1882 the gun carriages were temporarily reinforced so that the artillery could honour the Governor-General, the Marquis of Lorne, and H.R.H. Princess Louise on their visit to New Westminster. In 1883 disaster befell the one, relatively sound, field piece. On the eve of Victoria Day it was in its accustomed location opposite Albert Crescent. The **British Columbian** told the rest of the story: "On Wednesday night at 12 o'clock the citizens of New Westminster were startled by a heavy report of artillery which shook every building within the corporation. A good many people jumped out of bed in a state of bewilderment, and visions of dynamite and carnage flashed suddenly through many a muddled brain. It turned out that some miscreant had loaded the big gun at the battery with powder and ball and set it off in honour of the Queen's Birthday. The shot passed through the flagstaff, cutting it down, and the gun carriage was considerably smashed. The carriage needs no apology, however, for it was very rotten and scarcely fit for active service. The gun must have had an extra charge, for the report was fearfully loud. By reference to our advertising columns it will be seen that Capt. Pittendrigh, Commander of the Seymour Artillery, offers a reward of $20 for the rascals who committed this outrage upon the British flag, and insulted the dignity of the Queen."[13] Somehow, enough was salvaged from the debris and one gun carriage was reconstructed to allow the royal salutes to continue in subsequent years. The Northwest Rebellion of 1885 loosened the purse strings of Ottawa and some money for the rebuilding of the gun carriages was provided. Both howitzers were back in action, for the newspaper report of Victoria Day, 1888 stated "At noon a detachment of men from the artillery, under Capt. Bole, Lieut. McNaughten and Lieut. Mowat, fired a salute of 21 guns from the battery opposite the Crescent, in the presence of a large number of people...the men looked well and served the guns like veterans."[14] This was the last time when the unit's brass cannon were used to mark the queen's birthday.

In 1879 the Dominion Inspector of Artillery, Lieut. Col. T. Bland Strange, had suggested that the Seymour Battery become part of a future west coast brigade of artillery to be composed of four complete batteries. The New Westminster unit was eventually incorporated as No. 1 Battery of the new British Columbia Provisional Regiment of Garrison Artillery in October 1883. The regiment, whose headquarters were in Victoria, was given the more manageable name of British Columbia Brigade of Garrison Artillery (B.C.B.G.A.) in 1886. It was reasonable to suppose that what had long been denied to the independent, half-battery on the Fraser could not be withheld from it when it was part of a brigade. If that was the expectation of the New Westminster gunners, they were in for a disappointment. They were still stuck with their two, Crimean War howitzers.

When Captain William Norman Bole formally replaced George Pittendrigh as battery commander in January 1886, the acting Deputy Adjutant-General testified to the former commander's ability not only to keep the battery alive but also to build up its discipline and morale. "The very satisfactory condition of Captain Pittendreigh's (sic) Battery during the past two years -- last year the best and smartest corps in this District -- has been owing to the zeal and energy displayed by him in its behalf, and its condition...is deserving of the highest credit...how the officers and men managed to maintain interest in their work, with their obsolete weapons mounted on rotten carriages, I can hardly imagine."[15] For old soldiers, however, all changes in the traditional order of things are for the worse. On a winter's night in 1907 the future achivist of Vancouver, James Skitt Matthews, took down the reminiscences of W. Norman Bole, an Irish lawyer who had settled in New Westminster and had served with the militia artillery there.

The uniform of the Seymour Battery, Major Matthews was told,
> was that of the Royal Horse Artillery, and Judge Bole told me that while they did not wear the ornaments of the R.H.A. still there was no doubt that they were entitled to do so. It was, he said, a gorgeous looking affair, but the officers' great coats were cold. In a fine Irish brogue which he could assume at will, he said to me "And didn't I pay me foine farty dollars for the miserable thing." The men's coats were much better, and when I met him...that evening he was, as we walked, wearing one of the men's great coats which he said he had worn for over twenty years.

Such were the distinctions enjoyed by the battery as one of the territorial units of Great Britain. When their talk turned to the incorporation of the battery into the brigade in 1883, Judge Bole became bitter. "He assured me," continued Matthews, "that Capt. Pettindrigh (sic), who was afterwards its commander, made a great mistake when he arranged for the battery to be changed into the British Columbia Battery of Garrison Artillery. There was absolutely no reason other than an idea of Capt. Pettindrigh's which was that it would be quite a grand thing to be commander of No. 1 Battery of the B.C.B.G.A. But (in) making this change the seniority of the unity suffered greatly; Judge Bole said that had the corps continued it would have today (1907) been the senior militia corps in Canada...At the time of the Great Fire in Westminster in 1898 all Judge Bole's records, he said, and they were extensive, relating to the formation of the corps, were burnt."[16] This statement, which reveals the weakness of personal recollections when measured against contemporary documents, was not only unjust to George Pittendrigh; it also misrepresented the status of the Seymour Battery. The militia infantry at Victoria and New Westminster predated its formation and, at most, the Seymour Battery was the pioneer militia artillery corps in Western Canada.

Others in the Royal City shared Judge Bole's strong feelings about the seniority of their battery. In April 1893 the artillery brigade was reorganized as the British Columbia Battalion of Garrison Artillery with provision for six batteries. The existing ones were renumbered beginning, logically, with those closest to battalion headquarters in Victoria. The New Westminster battery would, in this scheme, become No. 4 rather than No. 1 Company. In a letter to the local commander, Capt. Thomas Owen Townley, the battalion C.O. Lieut. Col. Edward Gawlor Prior anticipated the objections to this apparent "demotion" of the battery.[17] Prior, a Member of Parliament who became Premier of the province, was described in his lifetime as "a typical, energetic business man of the present age -- methodical, systematic, aggressive, affable."[18] He was not a man who would back down to protests and protests there were against this change. The **Daily Columbian** of August 26th noted that when the alteration was first proposed it was "strenuously objected to by the officers and men of the Westminster battery, which is the senior militia organization of the Province, and rightly entitled to remain always at the head of the battalion. When Col. Prior was notified of the objection to the change, it was understood that he had decided to drop the matter. However, it appears otherwise..."[19] The local Member of Parliament added his voice to the chorus of disapproval and wired a protest to the Minister of Militia. There was talk of breaking up the company in protest but nothing came of it. Disbandment for quite another reason lay not far off.

In 1894 the old timers in the battery had a new cause for dissatisfaction. One newspaper described their response as a "mutiny and mimic war." The **Daily Columbian** of August 8th provided the most trustworthy account of the affair. "There is," it was reported, "a little trouble in No. 4 Co., B.C.B.G.A., which will result seriously for the corps if not settled soon. Inspection has been ordered for September 15th, and drill was called for last (Tuesday) night to prepare for the trying occasion. A large number of the men turned out, but owing to some dissatisfaction over the appointment of new officers no parade took place. The men, it appears, came to the conclusion that they would not serve under certain of the lately gazetted officers, and notified Lieut. (C.R.) Townley to that effect. Lieut. Townley, finding the men firm in the position they have assumed, announced that he would report the matter to Lieut.-Col. Prior, and in the meantime all parades were cancelled..the men say all they ask is that some of the officers should have had previous military experience. It is not on personal grounds that their objections are taken."[20] Under military law, the men could have been charged with insubordination and mutiny, but the Department of Militia took a more discreet course. By an order issued on September 8th, 1894, No. 4 Company was disbanded.

The justice of the junior ranks' action was indirectly acknowledged when the artillery company at New Westminster was reconstituted in April 1895. None of the provisional Second Lieutenants who had been gazetted in March 1894 reappeared in the general order of April 13th that revived the unit. The new officer commanding was John Andrew Forin, who had to be persuaded to accept the job. It is likely that the ringleaders of the protest, when known, were also prevented from re-enlisting in the unit. It was now Col. Prior's turn to express his vexation. The new officers behaved as though the New Westminster company were still an independent battery and they tended to ignore or bypass the battalion commander at Victoria. "God damn such men," wrote Prior in a private letter, "they are no more fit to be officers than I am to be a Bishop."[21]

The difficulties of controlling six dispersed companies from Victoria were resolved by dividing the B.C.B.G.A into two battalions, one of which had headquarters in Vancouver. Under the general order of 28th December, 1895, both battalions made up the 5th "British Columbia" Regiment, Canadian Artillery. In an apparent victory for the gunners of the Royal City, their unit in the Second Battalion was given the designation of No. 1 Company. Their victory was short-lived. In July 1899 the Second Battalion of the 5th Regiment, Canadian Artillery, became the Sixth Battalion, Rifles. There was one consolation in this conversion to infantry: it finally solved the problem of replacing the old, brass howitzers.

The citizens of New Westminster had already accommodated themselves to the absence of the guns on Victoria Day. In May 1889, a year after the last official royal salute, two junior officers of the battery, Lieutenants Mowat and Bonson, led others down to Thomas Ovens' blacksmithing and machine shop on Douglas Street. With two borrowed anvils, which were superimposed with a small gunpowder charge in between, the celebrants fired off a 21 "gun" salute.[22] Improvised salutes were not uncommon: in 1890 a wharf contractor at Victoria contrived a measured and solemn series of reports with dynamite and electrical fuses to honour the Duke of Connaught. At New Westminster the queen's birthday was allowed to pass quietly until 1892 when a group, including some militia veterans and members of the Hyack Fire Fighting Company, decided to imitate the example of the two subalterns. According to the **Daily Columbian** of May 25th, 1892, "The old timers... on the spur of the moment quickly made their preparations. At noon a Royal Salute of 21 guns was fired with anvils in front of Oven's machine shop, in old time style (sic)." The "veterans" were identified as "Capt. Peele (of the New Westminster Rifles), Messrs. Thos. Ovens, W.H. Vianen, James Stephens and John Buie."[23]

The anvil battery became an instant and popular "tradition" of New Westminster's May 24th celebrations. The group that did the firing was led by Captain Adolphus Peele and Thomas Ovens who, in addition to owning the anvils, was alderman and later mayor of the city. The new management of the **Daily Columbian** faithfully reported the group's yearly activities as well as its claims to antiquity. In 1893 the newspaper noted the birthday salute "fired by the Ancient and Honorable Pioneer Artillery Company, who since 1859 have never failed to honor Her Majesty in this manner." The firing technique was still to be perfected since "Bombardier Vianen was seriously wounded in the face by the twelfth explosion, and though the blood ran freely from the wound he declined to go to the rear for repairs, but stuck to his gun and fought it out with true Von Tromp courage until the last shot had been fired. Three cheers for the Queen and another for the Prince of Wales closed the celebration. The ancients then repaired to the nearest house of refreshment where Her Majesty's health was drunk with loyal enthusiasm."[24] The friends later styled themselves the Most Ancient and Honorable Hyack Anvil Battery and assumed such dignified offices as Commander and Swobber, Loader and Powder-Monkey, Left Hoister, Toucher-Off, Chalker-Up, and Spouter and Ginner-Up. The date of origin for the battery and its distinctive salute has been given as 1859, 1865 and 1871.[25] The first documented salute, however, was in 1889 and this group began in 1892. Nonetheless, the Hyacks, who are still active, can fairly claim to be the successors of the New Westminster Volunteers and the Seymour Battery who from 1867 to 1888 had saluted the queen's birthday with rifles and cannon. The two guns, in whose stead the anvils jump, sit silently on either side of the Simon Fraser memorial at the east end of New Westminster's Columbia Street.

CHAPTER 2

Sham Battles at Vancouver, 1859-1899

Burrard Inlet answered the Royal Navy's need for a large, ice-free harbour on the mainland of British Columbia. The freshwater anchorage at New Westminster was inaccessible to large warships and it was more exposed to attack from the south. Between the Fraser River and the inlet there was a heavily-wooded ridge that was traversed in the 1860's by an easily-defended trail. In 1859 Captain George H. Richards and Daniel Pender of H.M. sloop **Plumper** surveyed the harbour and the energetic Col. Richard Clement Moody R.E. continued their work. Included in the surveys were recommendations that certain lands be set aside as military and naval reserves for the future use and defence of the inlet. In the next decade fourteen areas were permanently or temporarily closed to civilian occupation. The naval reserves were located at Jericho, the area that is now Vancouver's central business district, and on both sides of the Port Moody arm of the inlet. The last was a secure and sheltered anchorage close to New Westminster, the capital of the mainland colony. Port Moody assumed even greater importance when it was chosen as the terminus of the Canadian Pacific Railway. The military reserves were not only located here but also at the obvious defensive points at the First Narrows and the outer entrance to the inlet. The location of these government reserves is shown on the accompanying map. Half of them were eventually opened to private landholders and the remainder were the basis of Greater Vancouver's extensive public parks. The ultimate credit for preserving such gems as Stanley Park, Jericho Beach and the University Endowment Lands does not belong to far-seeing politicians; it should be given to the naval and army officers who feared Russian and American aggression.

In July 1881 Col. Crossman R.E. and Commander Bourke of the Royal Navy submitted a joint report on the military and naval reserves of Burrard Inlet to the Inspector General of Fortifications in Britain. The building of a transcontinental railway that was to end on the inlet had revived interest in the protection of the harbour. The Crossman-Bourke Report has disappeared, but an abstract of its contents survives. The summary speaks of using the 500 acre reserve on the tip of Point Grey for siting "a battery of very heavy guns

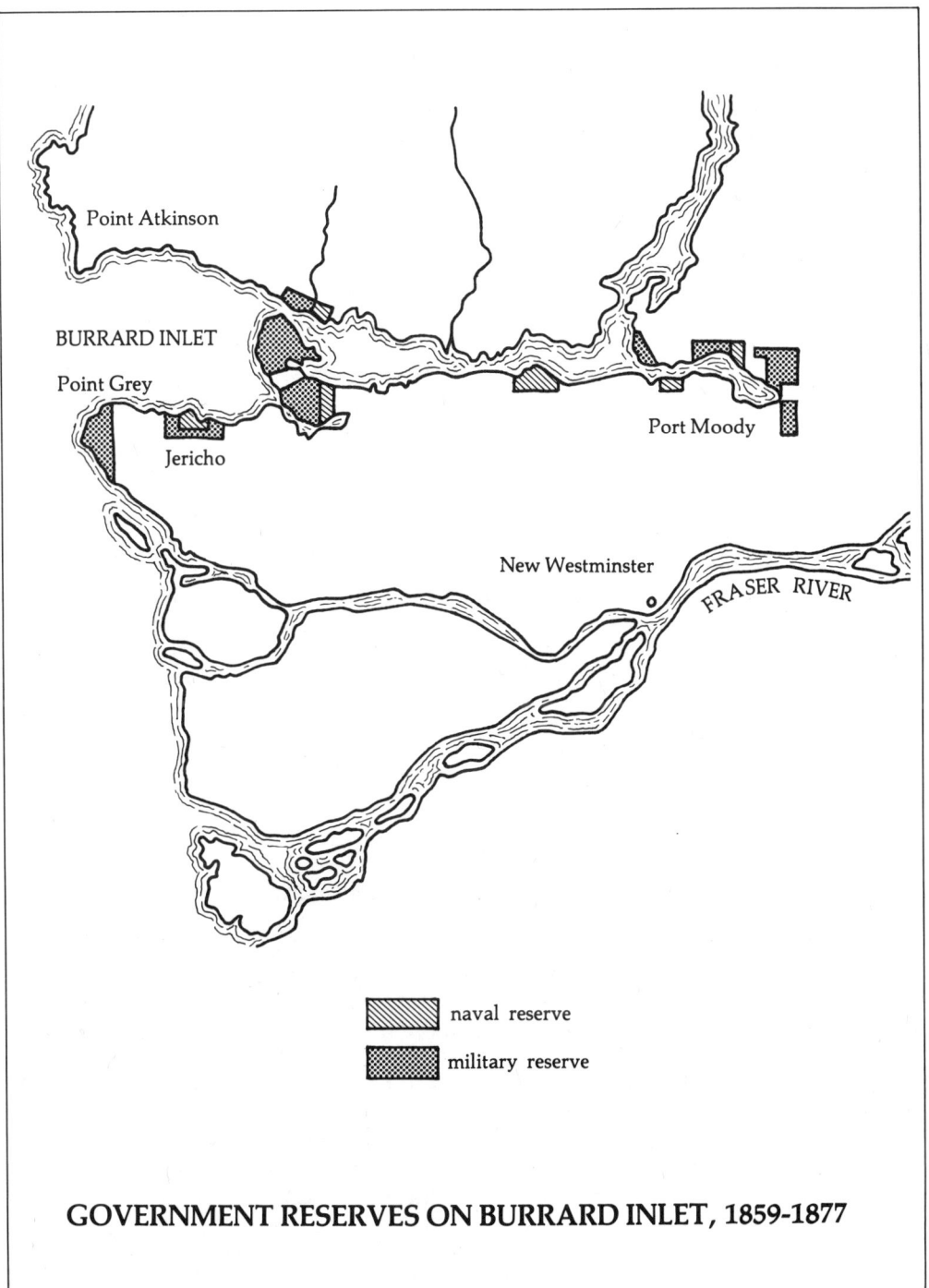

on the Northern corner" which would "with a work at Point Atkinson on the other side of the bay (which is not reserved) protect to some extent the anchorage in English Bay."[1] The West Coast of North America, however, had a minor place in the defence plans of the British Empire and the slender resources of the Royal Navy and the Canadian Department of Militia, which dealt with such matters, were devoted to the development and protection of the naval base at Esquimalt. This establishment on Vancouver Island, it could be argued, gave advanced protection to Burrard Inlet. It was also assumed that The Canadian Pacific Railway, completed in November 1885, would quickly deliver reinforcements from Eastern Canada in an emergency. As a consequence, the reserves around Vancouver Harbour experienced nothing more lethal before 1914 than the woodsman's axe. They were military in name alone.

When Rudyard Kipling arrived at the newly-incorporated City of Vancouver in 1889, he rejoiced at the sight of "the old flag" and the presence of "Englishmen who speak the English tongue correctly and with clearness, avoiding more blasphemy than is necessary." His recent passage through the United States coloured his view. Kipling marvelled too at the complete absence of defences for Vancouver's "almost perfect harbour." "My interest," he wrote, "was in the line -- the real and accomplished railway which is to throw actual fighting troops into the East some day when our hold of the Suez Canal is temporarily loosened. All that Vancouver wants is a fat earthwork fort upon a hill, -- there are plenty of hills to choose from, -- a selection of big guns, a couple of regiments of infantry, and later on a big arsenal...It is not seemly to leave unprotected the head-end of a big railway; for though Victoria and Esquimalt, our naval stations on Vancouver Island, are very near, so also is a place called Vladivostok, and though Vancouver Narrows (sic) are strait, they allow room enough for a man-of-war"[2] Alas, Vancouverites of that day were more concerned with the prospects of foreign trade and real estate sales. So Kipling acquired a vacant town lot but no converts to the cause of imperial defence.

The lack of defensive measures was not due to a total indifference to military matters. The residents of Burrard Inlet loved the dash and colour of uniforms, particularly the blue and red of the gunners. Robertson Ross' recommendation in 1872 that a rifle company be raised locally came to naught as did an 1884 proposal for an artillery battery. After the incorporation of Vancouver in April 1886 the residents' desire for their own militia unit was whetted by the sight of New Westminster's citizen soldiers in Vancouver's Dominion Day parades. In 1889 it was reported that the procession included "the artillery, 35 strong, under Lieut. Mowat, and accompanied by the New Westminster rifles' fife and drum band ...The military portion of the parade, and No. 1 battery B.G.A. in particular, was cheered repeatedly along the route."[3] On occasion the militiamen shared the approval of the crowds with the marines and "blue-jackets" of visiting British warships. Even the Knights of Labour supported the formation of a militia unit in Vancouver, provided the lower ranks could elect their officers. The military enthusiasm of the Vancouverites was evident in January 1893 when two hundred volunteered to help Hawaii's Queen Liliuokalani recover her throne from the Americans who had overthrown her government. The planned expedition foundered for want of money. Clearly, the time for the establishment of the city's first reserve unit had arrived.

When the British Columbia Battalion of Garrison Artillery was reorganized in April 1893, it was decided that a fifth company of the battalion should be raised in Vancouver. The man chosen for the job was the former commander of No. 1 Battery, Thomas Owen Townley, a barrister who later became mayor of the city. On June 12th, 1893, the **Daily World** reported that "Capt. T.O. Townley has been notified that authority has been delegated to him to raise a corps of garrison artillery in Vancouver of a strength of 100 men. The service rolls are now on their way from Ottawa, and he will start in to recruit as soon as they arrive." In a reference to past agitation for a local militia unit, the newspaper added "this settles the long vexed question."[4] To assist Capt. Townley's recruiting efforts, the militia gunners of Victoria and the band of "C" Battery (permanent force) from Esquimalt paraded in Vancouver on Dominion Day. The July 7th issue of the **News-Advertiser** advised those wishing to sign the recently-delivered service roll of the new company that they could do so at Capt. Townley's office "in the Court House between the hours of 4 and 5 each day during the next ten days. It will be necessary to have the requisite number of men enrolled before the clothing can be ordered, on account of the various sizes." These fortunates would be spared the loose-fitting attire issued to the Seymour Battery in 1878. The **Daily World** also informed prospective recruits that "other things being equal, the first signers will be given the preference in the first draft of non-coms. Of officers, the battery will have a major, a captain, two lieutenants and a subaltern...No one who is not in robust health, and who does not stand at least 5 ft. 6 in. in height, need apply for enlistment."[5] The service roll was also kept at a tobacco store at Cambie and Cordova streets for the enlistment of latecomers. Local hopes that the city would be given an independent company rather than a battalion sub-unit were not fulfilled, but otherwise the recruiters bubbled with optimism. The newspapers were informed that "Next year a suitable drill hall will be built here...It is expected that guns similar to those about to be placed at Esquimalt will be mounted here for annual firing and drill purposes, and Col. Prior hopes to have the whole battalion armed with Martini-Henry rifles. A suitable rifle range has been procured on the Government reserve midway between here and New Westminster."[6]

The uniforms and equipment of No. 5 Company (Vancouver) were received from Ottawa early in 1894 and were issued to the recruits on January 16th and 17th. The men were then sworn in. Captain Townley had been promoted to the rank of Major to command the company and his officers were Lieut. Charles Arthur Worsnop, Dominion Customs Surveyor; Lieut. Lacey C. Johnson, a master mechanic for the C.P.R.; Lieut. Charles Gardner-Johnson, a ship and insurance broker; and Lieut. W. "Tom" Boultbee, the manager of C. Gardner Johnson & Co. It can be seen that the militia officers were drawn from the professionals, civil servants and leading business families of the province. Since officers had to buy their own uniforms and accoutrements and they needed leisure time to perform their military duties, it was natural that most were well-to-do or self-employed. They were also of British ancestry, born either in Eastern Canada or Great Britain. The ethnic composition of the lower ranks was similar; of the 63 non-commissioned officers and men who attended the first drill parade, only two did not have British surnames. The cultural uniformity of Vancouver's first militia unit was related to the fact that the Canadian armed forces modelled themselves on those of Great Britain and their conception of patriotism was loyalty to the British Empire. The militia had a special appeal for those who prided themselves on their British heritage. This close association with the dominant social and economic group gave the citizen soldiers prestige in the community and they enjoyed being referred to by their militia rank.

The first routine order of No. 5 Company was issued by Major Townley on January 22nd and it read:

1. *The company will parade at the drill shed on Mondays, Tuesdays, Wednesdays and Thursdays at 8 p.m., until further notice.*
2. *The following promotions will take place:*

To be sergeant and acting sergeant-major: J.C. Cornish.
To be sergeants: Gunner H.T. Sharp, N. LaBranche, F. Boys.
To be corporals: Gunner J. Duff Stuart, G.A. Boult, John Turner
To be Bombardiers: Gunner F.W. Alexander, L.A. Martin.
(signed:) T.O. Townley, Major.

The drill hall was not the new structure that had been promised; it was the vacant Imperial Opera House on Pender Street, near the intersection with Abbott. It had been built in 1889 and was neither very imperial nor very operatic. It was a fifty foot wide, frame building not much different from other boom-town, commercial structures. Vancouver archivist, J.S. Matthews, recorded the fact that it was "a plain 'shop front' building, square in front, of ship lap, big windows with big panes...with a cornice, and painted red, barn red."[8] The main floor, which was reinforced after the government purchased the edifice, was used for drill while the theatre stage served as an instruction area for new recruits.

By springtime in 1894, the men of the Vancouver artillery company were sufficiently trained as infantrymen to risk a public display of their skills. Not all of the potential hazards had been taken into account. Witness the story contained in the **News-Advertiser** of May 10th:

FIRST PUBLIC APPEARANCE OF NO. 5 COMPANY, B.C.B.G.A.[9]

Last night the local company, No. 5 of the British Columbia Brigade of Garrison Artillery made their first appearance in public and with considerable credit to their officers and themselves. After falling in at the Armory, if the Imperial Opera House would condescend to pass by so military a title, the company marched over to Cordova Street, thence westward to the end of the pavement where the manual (of drill) was gone through.

This was somewhat interrupted by the efforts of one or two fellows, -- probably under the influence, -- this is certainly the most charitable view to take of them -- who attempted to take command both to the disgust and annoyance of both officers and men. The silly fellows were probably unaware that their childish pranks were of such a nature as to cause their instant arrest by a corporal's guard, and a free blanket and breakfast with other vags under the guardian eye of Mr. John Clough at the Police Station, with a consequent front seat at the Cadi's (magistrate's) morning levy. Happily for them, however, the officers of No. 5 Co. are somewhat long suffering and did not wish to mar the first appearance of their company by resorting to such extremities...

The various movements were completed in a most creditable manner and the many citizens who turned out as spectators are justly proud of Vancouver's first company. The march home was then made via Seymour and Richards streets. It is to be regretted that the muster was not a better one, only 60, or about two-thirds of the company's strength turning out.

Poor attendance at rehearsal parades is a constant problem in the militia and in May 1897 public notice was given that "Every man who wishes to go to Victoria in June must turn out...Those who shirk the drudgery of preparation cannot expect to take part in the excursion. There will be many Vancouver people there and the 'march past' and ceremonial drill will be closely watched, so the 2nd Batallion (sic) must go by like a "wall."[10]

As a reward for what had been achieved in the first months of 1894, Major Townley gave the men a complimentary trip to Nanaimo at the end of May. When the steamship **Cutch** reached its destination, the master was told that he had embarked more passengers than the law allowed. He quietly made up his mind as to who would be left behind. The ship cast off for the return journey leaving the astonished militiamen standing on the point. They were rescued after a few hours by the **Robert Dunsmuir**, whose captain was nearly as inflexible as that of the **Cutch**. He insisted on returning to his home port of New Westminster and from there the dejected gunners straggled home to Vancouver.

Diagonally across from the drill hall on Pender Street was the "gun shed," a smaller frame building with a dirt floor. Before 1895 the "guns" were dummy field pieces consisting of water or gas pipes on wheels. The gunners did their shooting with rifles at the Central Park Rifle Range. R. Frank Marrion, a licence inspector who was sworn in to the company in January 1894, recalled that the unit's two 64-pounder guns were received in about 1896. When interviewed in the 1930's, he said that "One of the guns had a wooden carriage, and we used that for repository work, mounting and dismounting. The other we used for elementary gun practice. We had a package of something or other to represent gunpowder, and we'd ram this into the gun. It had a long lanyard on it. Then we'd ram in the shot -- it weighed sixty-four pounds -- and it also had a rope loop. Then we would 'fire' the cannon, and pull out the shot and powder, and go through the operation again and again. No, we never had any accidents with the shot. Now and then a man would skin his fingers as he shoved the ball into the cannon, but usually they got to be pretty careful."[11]

One accident, in fact, did occur and with spectacular results. The event seems to have occurred in 1897 during gun drill in the armoury. The rope attached to the training shell became twisted and the shell jammed in the barrel of the muzzle-loading cannon. Tugging at the rope broke the line. Major J.S. Matthews picked up the story:

> No extractor was available at the time, and in vain was every persuasion used to recover the delinquent shot. Then some one suggested that it might be blown out with a gentle charge, and the idea was voted a good one. Some powder from an old stock of cartridges in the gallery was secured, and a little, just a very little, carefully poured down the touchhole. An unsuccessful attempt was made to discharge the gun, so a little more powder was used, but still no result. Then they said 'Oh pshaw, put something worth while down, a whole handful,' and down a whole handful went. The primer was properly adjusted, the gun crew stood at their posts in review order, the gun captain gave the command, and the gunlayer pulled the lanyard. There was a deafening roar, a huge cloud of white smoke, and the crashing of timbers told that an invisible something had bored a gapping hole in the wall, finally bringing up with a thud in the bushes beyond.
>
> The gun crew stood aghast. They were speechless with surprise. Terrified officers came rushing from all parts of the hall and explanations followed. The smoke cleared away, when, lo and behold, two 64 lb. shells with rope, rings and all disclosed themselves. One had gone clean through the wall while the other lay on the floor of the shed. The gun had been sent from headquarters with a shell in it which had not been previously discovered.

"No one," commented the writer, "was hurt, but some were badly frightened, and a hole was blown in the side of the drill hall through which a fox terrier could jump."[12]

Vancouver's military ambitions were not satisfied by the creation of one artillery company, especially since Victoria had three of her own. More men had presented themselves for enlistment in No. 5 Company than could be accommodated. With just two guns and no immediate prospect of a larger drill hall, the gunners had good reasons to resist expansion; instead, they welcomed the addition of another company. In October 1895, and with official approval, No. 6 Company (Vancouver) was organized with Captain C.A. Worsnop as commander. When the 5th "British Columbia" Regiment, Canadian Artillery, was reorganized into two battalions on September 29th, 1896, the Vancouver units became No. 2 and 3 Companies of the Second Battalion. Lieut. Col. Townley, as he now was, served as battalion commander until June 1897 when the demands of his own affairs obliged him to hand the position over to C.A. Worsnop. Remembering his troubles in New Westminster, Col. Prior appreciated the quality of the officers recruited by Townley. "My dear Townley," wrote Prior in a letter of January 10th, 1895, "It is **most** encouraging to me to see you able to get such splendid fellows around you as you have done -- the corps cannot help but to be a success with such officers."[13]

The two battalions of the 5th Regiment came together at least twice a year. On Dominion Day the regiment paraded through Vancouver, often with detachments of the Royal Navy, to the Cambie Street grounds where a march past and review would be held. On Victoria Day the joint muster was elsewhere. R.F. Marrion remembered that "nearly every year, on May 24, we would go to Vancouver Island for manoeuvres with other British Columbia companies...Then, at these manoeuvres, the warships at Esquimalt would land men and participate. We usually had target practice with the big guns at Macaulay Plains, firing at moving targets."[14] Sham battles often followed the joint reviews and they attracted a large civilian audience. On May 26th, 1896, crowds came out of Victoria to Macaulay Point to see the conflict and one overloaded streetcar passed through Point Ellice Bridge. Over fifty people drowned in this tragedy. On Victoria Day 1899 the regiment presented its martial spectacle at Nanaimo. This was a happy contrast with the appearance of the militia at Nanaimo in 1877 to assist the sheriff in evicting striking coal miners from company housing.

Vancouver was the site of at least two mock battles. In September 1896 the two Vancouver units and one Victoria company held the hill near the foot of Denman Street against a spirited attack by another Victoria company with sailors and marines of the British navy. Dominion Day 1899 was the occasion for the last and most elaborate fray staged by the 5th Regiment. The plan was that:[15]

> after review the 1st Battalion, composed of the three Victoria companies will proceed to Stanley Park by boat, rowed by blue-jackets of the fleet in port, and attempt to reach the City via the bridge at Coal Harbour. The 2nd Battalion, composed of the New Westminster Company and the two Companies of Vancouver will march via Georgia, Burrard, and Alberni Streets and take up their position south of the bridge to protect the City. A hot engagement will then take place for this important position. Two (naval) 7-pounders will also be placed in position at the top of Robson Street hill, from which point they will greet the invaders with a storm of shot and shell.
>
> Meanwhile the Navy boats will have returned to the ships (H.M.S. Pheasant, Icarus and Phaeton) and will then proceed to land detachments of marines and blue-jackets at the Point...Major Lacy R. Johnson will be in command of the Mainland detachments.

The public was rather disappointed by the event for, as the **News-Advertiser** explained, "the smokeless powder, and the fighting line being under cover as much as possible, made it rather unreal to the uninitiated, who evidently expected the contending armies to meet and fight hand-to-hand in the middle of the bridge, and possibly fling a few of each other over the side."[16] There was no lack of realism in March 1908 when the Duke of Connaught's Own Rifles re-enacted a battle against the South African Boers. Someone mixed live rounds with the blanks and the "Boers" suffered six wounded and one perforated Stetson hat.

In addition to the regular reviews and sham battles, there were other memorable events in the short history of the mainland companies of the 5th Regiment. In May 1897 two gunners were dispatched to London to march with the Canadian Battalion in the procession for Queen Victoria's Diamond Jubilee. The units also turned out a guard of honour for Japan's Count Ito as he passed through Vancouver on his way to the same event. In 1899 farewell was said to those who left to fight in Britain's war in South Africa. When, in 1898, the Victoria battalion had been invited to join the American Independence Day celebrations at Seattle, Col. Prior, with great munificence, paid the travel expenses of the second battalion. In Seattle on July 4th the colonel, mounted on a bay charger, led the two battalions as they paraded to the tune of "Marching through Georgia." "Wild Cheers for Britain" exclaimed the **Post Intelligencer** while the **Seattle Times** trumpeted "The Canadians Help Us to Celebrate Nation's Birthday...Parade Demonstrates the Principles of Anglo-Saxon Unity." Pride of race was fired by an announcement that in the United States' war against Spain Admiral Cervera's fleet had just been defeated off Santiago de Cuba. Major Matthews, who witnessed the parade, recalled that "there was a huge demand for buttons and badges from the Canadian uniforms as souvenirs...and in the early hours after dawn the tired, worn, but happy wreck of Colonel Prior's command, buttonless, sleepy, but with few absentees, tried to pull itself together on the embarkation dock, ready to return home, after one of the most enjoyable, eventful and historic visits it may ever undertake."[17]

The Vancouver militia gloried in the brass-buttoned, blue artillery uniform. It was a smart outfit trimmed with yellow on the pillbox cap and tunic, with a scarlet stripe on the trousers and set off with white gloves and a white belt ornamented with a brass buckle. The spiked helmet worn on ceremonial occasions was also white and bore the Royal Artillery crest. The Second Battalion had achieved some distinction as riflemen in shooting contests. As gunners, their value to the defence of Canada was less certain. In the spring of 1899 plans were afoot to reorganize the militia in British Columbia so that it would complement the permanent force detachments at Victoria-Esquimalt. Of the 5th Regiment, only the Victoria-based, First Battalion would continue as artillery. The mainland battalion was to be converted to an infantry unit. The regimental C.O. quashed a suggestion that some of the gunners might serve as a pioneer corps to aid the navy. "The men of both battalions are largely drawn from young men in offices and general places of business," he wrote, "the common labourer has a very small representation in the militia of this district."[18]

The officers of the Second Battalion doggedly fought the conversion of their organization from artillery to infantry. Paper salvoes were fired in the direction of Victoria and Ottawa to preserve the unit and its small, newly-formed school of gunnery. "An artilleryman," wrote Lieut. Col. C.A. Worsnop to his superior in Victoria, "is a man of brains who thinks for himself, not a mere machine...What a waste of the training my officers and men have spent so many hours absorbing...Vancouver is unsuitable for infantry training, because of its heavy timber, dense undergrowth and fallen trees. This would prevent anything like extended order, and would confine operations to roads."[19] Unlike the sham conflicts, this was a real battle and it was being lost.

The battle against change was ended by the militia order of July 20th, 1899, which transformed the Second Battalion into the Sixth Battalion, Rifles. The publication of the order in Vancouver, observed the **News-Advertiser** of August 6th, "is a very severe test of the discipline existing in the corps,...The officers are very reticent...under the circumstances they must either obey without a word of protest, or resign their commissions in the service they have given much time and study to, and in which they have a strong interest." Part of that interest involved an expensive uniform which each officer would have to replace with the plainer black and dull green of a rifle regiment. Not all of the gunners were reticent about their feelings. The newspaper quoted a bit of doggerel, whose author was not named, that expressed the distaste of an artilleryman for that drab attire he would now have to wear.[20]

> *"From the radiant brilliance of brass and blue*
> *To the dull dead black of shoddy and glue,*
> *The cheapest cloth of the uniform-makers,*
> *For the Sixth Battalion of Undertakers."*

The battalion was somewhat mollified when the Duke of Connaught became its Colonel-in-Chief and the rifles were recast as the Sixth Regiment (Duke of Connaught's Own Rifles). It was not until 1920 that a militia artillery regiment was re-established in Vancouver. In the interim militia recruits on the Lower Mainland had the choice of a Field Ambulance, Engineer or Army Service Corps detachment and four infantry regiments: the 104th New Westminster, the 72nd Seaforth Highlanders, the 11th Irish Fusiliers, and the 6th D.C.O.R. When the future King George V opened the Beatty Street Armouries in Vancouver in September 1901 -- this was the new drill hall promised in 1893 -- it was the 6th Battalion, Rifles that took possession. Outside the building are two 64-pounders, a memento of the gunners who formed the city's first militia unit.

In the 1930's the mainland companies of the old 5th B.C.B.G.A. were remembered with nostalgia. "The boys of the old brigade" held reunions in 1937, 1938 and 1940 and exchanged memories of comrades and youthful escapades. Some stories grew with retelling: a former powder-boy of the Seymour Battery, in successive accounts of his enlistment, pushed the date farther and farther back into the mists of antiquity. "Remember when the sergeant bawled us out for carrying umbrellas while wearing the Queen's uniform?" asked one ex-gunner of his fellows in 1940[21] In the light of the Boer War and the two world conflicts that followed, those days in the 1890's when the men of Vancouver and New Westminster paraded in gaudy uniforms and fought mock battles in which no one died seemed like the innocence of childhood.

CHAPTER 3

Cruisers Loose in the Pacific

Germany's invasion of Luxembourg and Belgium provoked the British declaration of war on August 4th, 1914. It took this event, half a world away, to jolt the British Columbians out of their happy complacency. They looked upon the war in Europe as their own for membership in the British Empire gave English-speaking Canadians a more cosmopolitan outlook than their insolationist neighbours to the south. The men of the province volunteered in extraordinary numbers to fight for king and empire. Those people of German and Austrian origin, even when they were British subjects, were suspected of disloyalty; this was the ugly aspect of wartime patriotism. "I must say," wrote a Canadian colonel involved in the apprehension of enemy aliens, "that if men of distinctly foreign appearance and terribly foreign names will ask awkward questions of B.C. horsemen (mounted police) they must expect arrest."[1] On Point Grey the militia infantry guarded the Canadian government wireless station and the Pacific cable station against enemy saboteurs. The real danger came, not from foreign agents, but from seaward.

Count Maximilian von Spee's China squadron based at Tsingtao was perceived as the greatest threat to British Columbia. The squadron consisted of "two powerful armoured cruisers; and of three modern-type light cruisers, the **Emden, Nurnberg,** and **Leipzig,** besides smaller vessels."[2] The German colonies of Samoa, the Carolines, and other islands provided these warships with friendly ports throughout the western Pacific Ocean. The **Leipzig** was known to be on patrol off the Mexico-California coast while the **Nurnberg** was imagined to be equally close at hand. These were formidable cruisers built in 1904-1905, armed with ten 4.1-inch calibre guns each, and capable of a speed of 23 knots.

The coastal defences and naval forces in British Columbia were a weak shield against an attack by the German cruisers. Begun in 1878, the Victoria-Esquimalt batteries were improved in the 1890's by the addition of modern, breech-loading 6-inch guns and quick-firing twelve-pounders. The complementary long-range, 9.2-inch battery on Signal Hill was still incomplete in 1914. The gun barrels had been allowed to rust in a ditch for a few years until public protests forced resumption of construction. The Canadian government, which had assumed responsibility for the batteries and naval base in 1906, was indifferent to the defences. The decline in the naval protection was due to the change in the Dominion government in 1911. Sir Robert Borden of the Conservatives did not wish to develop Laurier's "tin-pot navy;" he favoured cash contributions to the Royal Navy which, in return, would protect Canada. It was a contestable assumption.

The warships stationed at Esquimalt comprised the light cruiser **Rainbow**, of 3,600 tons displacement, that had been acquired as a training vessel for the Canadian Naval Service, and two sloops-of-war on loan from the Royal Navy. **Rainbow** had been built in 1891 and was no longer capable of achieving her designed speed of 17.25 knots. The newer sloops **Algerine** and **Shearwater,** each of about 1,000 tons displacement, were even slower and they lacked radio communications. They were cruising off the shores of Mexico to protect or evacuate any British subjects who might be endangered by that country's civil war. These three ships all had a mixed armament that was a handicap to coordinated gunfire and accurate ranging. Each sloop had four 4-inch calibre and four 3-pounder guns. **Rainbow** possessed two 6-inch guns supported by an array of 4.7-inch and 12-pounder guns as well as torpedo tubes. She had no high explosive shells for the main guns. Unlike her sister ship **Niobe** at Halifax, **Rainbow,** though undermanned, was ready for the sea in the summer of 1914. That was really an accident since she had only been readied for a patrol of the northern seal fishery. She was, however, available in July to compel the **Komagata Maru,** carrying 350 unwanted East Indian immigrants, to leave Vancouver and Canadian waters. The public was largely ignorant of **Rainbow's** shortcomings and people naively believed that her extra length and her 6-inch guns made **Rainbow** a match for any German cruiser. The principal regret was that there was only one of her and she could not be everywhere at once.

As the war with Germany drew nigh, the July 30th issue of the **Vancouver Daily Province** asked "Will Rainbow Stay As Coast's Sole Defence?" The sealing patrol had not yet been cancelled. The newspaper went on to explain its apprehension:[3]

> *If Great Britain and Germany are drawn into a European war, on opposite sides, what is going to happen to British Columbia? How will this defenceless province protect herself from raids by hostile cruisers?...A week or two ago the Komagata Maru was anchored in Burrard Inlet. She was only an old Japanese tramp carrying 352 hostile Sikhs, Hindus and Mohammedans, but she baffled the authorities, stirred up public feeling, beat off a force of police...It was an object lesson which has not been forgotten for if the Komagata Maru had been equipped with a few quick-firers she could have commanded Vancouver's waterfront...Vancouver has no fortifications. There are no batteries which could be used for defence...A hostile warship would not need to pass through the Narrows, which could be mined. She could ride out in the gulf and shell the port without any risk to herself. Vancouver could be bombarded, Nanaimo, Union Bay and Ladysmith lose their coal stocks, Prince Rupert wiped out and the small coastal villages raided and the people of the Pacific coast would have no means of fighting back except through the militia regiments. But infantry ashore are hopelessly out of action against a naval force with long range guns...Victoria has a smart force of militia gunners who are exercised in big-gun firing, but it is doubtful if the Esquimalt forts could hold a hostile squadron from passing up the straits. Once past Esquimalt the raiding cruisers would find themselves unopposed.*

New Westminster in the 1860's, seen from across the Fraser River.

Credit: New Westminster Public Library.

New Westminster in about 1898.

Credit: New Westminster Public Library.

The Seymour Battery of Garrison Artillery at "The Battery" southeast of Albert Crescent in New Westminster. This photograph was taken between 1878, when the men acquired spiked helmets, and 1886 when the helmets were replaced by busbies. Note the ill-fitting uniforms and the reinforcement of the wheel on the left hand gun.
Credit: New Westminster Public Library.

Captain Thomas Owen Townley (seated, centre, left) with the officers and non-commissioned officers of the New Westminster battery of the B.C. Brigade of Garrison Artillery in about 1892.
Credit: New Westminster Public Library.

The Non-Commissioned Officers of No. 5 (Vancouver) Company, British Columbia Brigade of Garrison Artillery, in May 1894: (left to right) Standing: Cpl. John Turner, Cpl. Joseph J. Hillier, Cpl. James Duff-Stuart, Bdr. E.J. Crickmay; Seated: Sgt. H.J. Sharp, Sgt. Major J.C. Cornish of "C" Battery, Sgt. Napoleon LaBranche, Sgt. G.A. Boult; Lying: Bdr. Albert Martyn, Col. Fred W. Alexander, Bdr. J. Reynolds Tite.
Credit: Vancouver City Archives.

The Officers of the Second Battalion, 5th Regiment, Canadian Garrison Artillery in 1896: (left to right) Standing: Capt. C.C. Bennett, Lieut. J. Reynolds Tite, _____, Lieut. Charles Arthur Worsnop; Dr. A.M. Robertson, Lieut. Charles Gardner-Johnson; Seated: Capt. J.C. Whyte (?), Major Thomas Owen Townley; Lying: Lieut. Lacey R. Johnson, Lieut. H.C. Akroyd, Lieut. F.W. Boultbee.   Credit: Vancouver City Archives

En Route to their Last Sham Battle: The companies of the B.C.B.G.A., preceded by their band, marching down Vancouver's Cordova Street on Dominion Day in 1899.
Credit: Vancouver City Archives.

A Firing Team of the Second Battalion, C.G.A., under Lieut. H.C. Akroyd at the Central Park Rifle Range on Thanksgiving Day, 1897. The men were armed with the long .303 Lee-Enfield rifle.

Credit: Vancouver City Archives.

With a band playing and with an audience of boys and adults, the 5th Regiment, Canadian Artillery, was inspected by an admiral from the visiting British naval squadron at Vancouver's Cambie Street Grounds on Dominion Day, 1897.
Credit: Vancouver City Archives.

Annual mess dinner of the Vancouver Companies of the Second Battalion, 5th Regiment, Canadian Artillery, in the former Imperial Opera House on Pender Street on January 26th, 1898. The stage area is behind the flags. On the wall are illustrations of bayonet drill.
Credit: Vancouver City Archives.

A sentry of the 6th Regiment (Duke of Connaught's Own) Rifles stands outside the Beatty Street Armoury in 1911. Beside him is one of the two muzzle-loading, 64-pounder guns issued to Vancouver's first militia unit in 1895. The other artillery piece had a wooden carriage.

Credit: Vancouver City Archives.

Naval volundeers under Lieut. Mock with the two 4-inch calibre guns on Stanley Park's Siwash Point in 1914.
Credit: Vancouver City Archives.

60-pounder guns of the type manned by the Cobourg Heavy Battery on Point Grey in 1914.
Credit: Peter N. Moogk.

Men of the 15th Field Brigade, Canadian Artillery, firing a 60-pounder gun at Sarcee Camp in the 1920's. The weapon is a full recoil.
Credit: Major R.V. Stevenson.

An Experiment in Mechanized Artillery in 1928: with trucks leased from the Terminal Cartage Company, the 5th Medium Battery prepares to leave its home in the Horseshow Building on Georgia Street for a weekend exercise.
Credit: Major J.G. Chutter.

The training cruiser H.M.C.S. Rainbow in Vancouver harbour in about 1914.
Credit: Vancouver City Archives.

Men of the 5th Battery go through gun drill with a 60-pounder at the Bessborough Armouries in about 1937.

Credit: 15th Field Artillery Regiment, R.C.A.

Officers and men of the 31st Field Battery, 15th Brigade, at Sarcee Camp in 1934. In the front row, starting with the second figure and going from left to right, are Sgt. Charlie Smith, Lieut. Jack Overholt, Lieut. Norm Smith, Capt. Gordon Y.L. Crossley, Major J.E. Piercy, Lieut. Theo DuMoulin, Pte. Dooley Sutherland, and Sgt. Tommy Packenham.

Credit: 15th Field Artillery Regiment.

The Bessborough Armouries on West 11th Avenue were built by a private association in 1932-33 for the militia artillery.

Credit: Peter N. Moogk.

Stanley Park Battery in September 1941: the roofs of the main camp can be seen on the left; a wire and board fence encloses the gun battery; and one shoreline searchlight emplacement is located on the right.

Credit: Public Archives of Canada, National Photography Collection.

Stanley Park Battery: (Top, left to right) The Battery Commander's position was on the top level of the concrete O-Pip; which on the outside was camouflaged with scrim and a painted evergreen tree. On its roof was the signals hut where a suicide occurred. (Below) men of the 31st Heavy Battery pose in front of one of the guns in 1940; some were still boys while others were First War veterans. Their sleeping quarters were at the Third Beach camp; the door to the Sergeants' Mess was labelled "Lovers' Walk."

Credit: Fort Rodd Hill National Historic Park and Harry Mangles.

Narrows North Fort in September 1941: the camp is under the bridge while the concrete "gantry" stands apart and to the left; the guns were originally located on the gravel spit at the river mouth.

Credit: Public Archives of Canada, National Photography Collection.

The flood at Narrows North in October 1939: a car ploughs through the water in the upper left; gunners wade about between the half-finished shacks of the camp.

Credit: Department of National Defence.

Installing the 12-pounder guns on the roof of the "gantry" at Narrows North in October 1939.
Credit: Department of National Defence.

Narrows North in 1942: from the "gantry" a 12-pounder fires a stopping round at a fishing boat and holes a Fort-class freighter instead.
Credit: Fort Rodd Hill National Historic Park and the Vancouver Maritime Museum.

This sense of being open to a sudden, unopposed naval attack would explain why, at the beginning of the war, many people transferred their funds and valuables to inland and American banks. One Victoria family went so far as to prepare their cemetery vault as an emergency shelter.

The first defensive measures of the war against the apparent threat to British Columbia were taken by the provincial government with an eye to strengthening the naval forces on the west coast. On July 29th, the same day that the British Admiralty sent out a "warning telegram" to all naval units, a meeting occurred at Victoria's Union Club. This unscheduled gathering included Mr. J.V. Paterson, the president of the Seattle Construction and Drydock Company, and Captain W.H. Logan, Surveyor to the London Salvage Association. In the course of their conversation Paterson let it be known that his shipyard had two submarines that had been constructed for Chile, but which might be available for sale to Canada. Chile had agreed to pay U.S. $818,000 for them and she was now slightly in arrears in completing the payment. The Chileans were unhappy about the excess weight of the vessels for their endurance was thereby reduced. The availability of the submarines was communicated to Sir Richard McBride, the Premier of the province, and through Logan he enquired about the purchase price. On August 3rd Paterson offered them at U.S. $575,000 a piece on a take it or leave it basis. He was asking for $332,000 more than the Chileans would have paid and the Canadians were in no position to dicker. Time was running out. War was a near certainty and the declaration against Germany would lead to a statement of neutrality by the United States and a consequent end of American arms sales to belligerents. Premier McBride knew this and, without the prior consent of Ottawa or his own legislature, he agreed to pay the full amount of $1,150,000 out of provincial funds.

On the night of August 4th the two submarines manned by company crews slipped out of Puget Sound for a dawn rendezvous near Trial Island, outside the three mile limit of both nations. A retired British naval officer and the chief engineer from Esquimalt inspected the vessels and, after handing over the provincial government's cheque, they raised the white ensign over the submarines. The vessels' approach took Esquimalt by surprise. "The unheralded arrival of the submarines caused much excitement," wrote the historian Gilbert N. Tucker, "Many of the people in Esquimalt concluded that the enemy was upon them. The examination vessel on duty outside ran hastily into the harbour, with the lanyard of her siren tied to the rail and the siren sounding an uninterrupted alarm. The shore batteries, which were manned by the Army and which had not, apparently, been warned, telephoned to the Dockyard before opening fire, in order to find out whether or not any submarines were expected." On the same day naval headquarters wired Victoria "Prepare to purchase submarines. Telegraph price." The reply was "Have purchased submarines."

Until the Dominion government took over responsibility for the submarines and transferred them to the Admiralty on August 7th, British Columbia had its own navy and was the only province since confederation to enjoy this privilege. The vessels were briefly known as Paterson and McBride, in honour of the builder and the buyer, before they were officially christened CC1 and CC2. This identified them as Canadian ships approximating the British C-class submarines. They were armed with 18-inch diameter torpedoes and their presence was well-publicized as a deterrent to the Germans. CC1 and CC2 remained on the west coast until June 21st, 1917 when they sailed for Halifax to help combat the menace of Germany's U-boats in the Atlantic.

Another, not as well known, contribution to the defence of British Columbia in 1914 was made by three fishing-boats leased by the Admiralty from the Anglo-British Columbia

Packing Company. The **Laurel Leaf, Holly Leaf** and **Ivy Leaf** became torpedo boats of a sort. Colin H. Crickmay, who was fifteen at the time, remembered that the "fishing smacks" were fitted "with a pair of torpedo tubes, one suspended on each side just above the water; these small boats patrolled local waters with instructions to close to pointblank range with an enemy ship and fire the torpedoes."[5]

With the province's defences bolstered by the acquisition of two submarines, **Rainbow** was ordered to steam southward to screen the two sloops from the **Leipzig**. The instructions received by Commander Walter Hose of **Rainbow** and dated August 5th were "Do your utmost to protect Algerine and Shearwater, steering north from San Diego. Remember Nelson and the British Navy. All Canada is watching."[6] The cruiser could not find the sloops with whom she had no radio contact. After coaling in San Francisco, **Rainbow** turned northward for her home port. The crew stripped the cruiser for action by tearing out much of the inflammable woodwork and throwing it overboard. When this debris washed up on the shores of California, it was assumed that the plucky old cruiser had met **Leipzig** and had gone to the bottom of the sea. There were also erroneous reports of gunfire off the Oregon coast. **Leipzig** did not follow the British and Canadian vessels farther north than Cape Mendocino. **Rainbow** caught up with the **Shearwater** on the 13th and together they entered Esquimalt that morning. **Algerine** was retrieved on the 15th. "Leipzig Has Again Headed South: Marine Defenders of Vancouver Are Safe" sighed the **Daily Province.**

False alarms were the order of the day, though the odd report proved to be true. **Nurnberg**, which everyone had assumed to be in the neighbourhood, appeared in the Hawaiian Islands. On September 7th a party from the German cruiser landed on Fanning Island and destroyed the shore installations for the Canada-Australia cable. The cable was a vital link in the "All-Red Line" of imperial communications championed by Canada's Sir Sanford Fleming. It was also reported that on August 17th **Leipzig** had taken on coal at San Francisco. While in harbour, her captain declared "we will engage the enemy whenever and wherever we meet him."[7] The Americans, however, would only supply enough coal to permit the warship to reach the nearest German possession. Far from repair facilities, it was not in the interest of **Leipzig** to risk damage in naval combat. This would end her career as a commerce raider. Unknown to Britain and her allies, the cruiser sailed on a southerly course to rejoin von Spee's squadron near Easter Island. For several weeks afterward the ghost of the **Leipzig** continued to haunt the minds of the British Columbians.

Leipzig's withdrawal from the North American coast was a wise move for the naval forces stationed at Esquimalt were being constantly built up. Japan, an ally of Britain since 1911, declared war on Germany on August 23rd and her heavy cruiser **Izumo** reached British Columbia two days later. The **Daily Province** described **Izumo** (whose name was rendered as Idzumo or Adzuma) as "a fighting vessel of 9438 tons displacement and has as armament, four 8-inch, twelve 6-inch, twelve 3-inch, eight 1.8-inch guns and five torpedo tubes. The vessel was a prize captured by the Japanese in the late war with Russia."[8] Her band gave the Canadian troops leaving Vancouver for the European front a rousing send-off. The battle cruiser H.M.A.S. **Australia** went in search of the **Nurnberg** and at the end of August the modern, light cruiser H.M.S. **Newcastle** arrived at Esquimalt. These powerful warships then went off to await von Spee near the entrance to the Panama Canal. **Rainbow** was left behind to comfort the coastal communities of northern British Columbia with her presence.

The rapidly-changing naval situation had not diverted attention away from land defences. The want of artillery on the Lower Mainland had been noted and, as before, local initiative went ahead of the Dominion government. On August 10th, two serviceable 4-inch calibre guns were requested from Esquimalt and they were delivered to Siwash Point in Vancouver's Stanley Park by H.M.S. **Shearwater**. The point near Siwash Rock was one hundred feet above the water and it commanded English Bay. With the removal of more trees from the line of fire, the battery could command the First Narrows. Working without a break, volunteers constructed two sunken platforms of 12 inch by 12 inch timbers overlaid with steel plates. The gun mountings were bolted to these plates. The positions were screened on the back and sides by earthworks. Similar batteries were erected at Seymour Narrows to cover the northern entrance to the Strait of Georgia. The Stanley Park guns were ready for action on August 15th and were test-fired on the 18th.[9]

In the absence of local militia gunners, the weapons on Siwash Point were served by ratings of the newly-organized Royal Canadian Volunteer Naval Reserve under the command of Lieut. Mock, a gunnery officer from **Rainbow**. His third officer was Sub-Lieutenant Eddie A. Lucas, a prominent city barrister who was later nicknamed "Admiral Lucas" in honour of his naval service. His recollections of 1914 were recorded by Arthur Mayse twenty-four years later. "Admiral Lucas" remembered the construction of the concrete-lined ammunition dump which, with the remains of a tree-top lookout, can still be seen on the point. He recalled that "two tents were pitched, one for the officers and another for the men, and in this makeshift barracks, the garrison remained until the threat of attack faded late in the year." Overly-curious citizens were arrested by the sentries and were interrogated in case they were enemy agents.

A second battery was established by the army on the northwest side of Point Grey in early September, 1914. The militia gunners involved came from the Cobourg Heavy Battery of Ontario. As "Admiral Lucas" told it, their 60-pounder field guns "were rushed by rail from Ontario and dragged into position in West Point Grey...The land battery arrived on a sweltering day in September, a militia major in command. Drawn by trucks, the gun carriages rumbled through downtown streets and out to Point Grey, where positions had been prepared, about half a mile east of the present 'washout gulley.'" When the guns reached their destination the soldiers discovered what they believed was an act of sabotage. "As the battery was being rolled into position, it was found that one of the hard steel breechblocks had been cracked clean across. 'That was no accident,' was the major's comment, 'only a man who knew how to destroy steel could have done that.' A local welder and electrician undertook to repair the block, making an all-night job of it, and both guns were ready for action next day."[10]

The arrival of the heavy guns of the Cobourg Battery gave impetus to a movement to form an artillery section in the Vancouver Volunteer Reserve or Home Guard. The first reference to the Home Guard was in an August 11th report of an interview with the local Member of Parliament, Mr. H.H. Stevens. Mr. Stevens acknowledged "a letter from Sir Robert Borden conveying the assuring intelligence that every precaution is being taken to safeguard the city and port of Vancouver." The newspaper added that "In connection with the question of local defense the suggestion that a home guard be formed in Vancouver is meeting with hearty endorsation. There are a large number of ex-army men in the city who have not joined the colors and the idea would be for them to undertake the training of citizens too old for active service and others who would like to take a share in the defense of the country in case of invasion but whose ties will not permit them to leave the city. A similar proposal has been urged that some guns be secured and corps trained in artillery practice."[11] This activity in Vancouver was reminiscent of the volunteer movement at New Westminster in 1866.

A thousand men volunteered for service in the Home Guard and the original plan was to divide them into calvary and infantry units. The idea of an artillery section was not dead. On September 5th it was noted that "upon glancing over the roll the committee in charge of the movement notices a large number of men whose previous service had been in the artillery, either garrison, field or horse, and it was suggested to Major McKay that he might get these men together and submit a proposition for forming an artillery section." An organizational meeting was held by the ex-gunners on Friday, September 4th and arrangements were made for gunnery lectures after "the usual infantry drill" of the volunteers. The artillery section had no weapons of its own and the venture depended on obtaining the use of the Cobourg Battery's field pieces. The newspaper report of the 5th added that "negotiations are now in progress whereby it is hoped that the artillery section will be given gun drill on the heavy battery station at Point Grey."[12]

There was no lack of enthusiasm for the artillery section. On September 8th "over fifty ex-gunners" paraded at the old Pender Street drill hall and more recruits were being enrolled by Major McKay who was still "making arrangements for lectures on gunnery and also drills on the five-inch guns at Point Grey." In addition to former artillerymen of the regular armies of Britain and Canada, the section was said to contain "ex-members of such well-known volunteer batteries as the Honourable Artillery Company, and former soldiers from other branches of the service."[13] On September 10th Col. C.A. Worsnop, who now commanded the Volunteer Reserve, inspected the section in its new home, "a spacious warehouse on Richards Street, between Drake and Pacific." Only fourteen of the eighty-six men on parade had had no previous military experience.[14] The last published report on the unit appeared on the 17th and described another parade as well as the appointment of "half-company commanders: J.M. Stewart, G.E. Milne, H.E. Boorman, W.N. Bainbridge, E.J. Pumphrey, A.H. Stewart, A.C.N. Mackay, G.P. Peroune, A.N. Daykin."[15] Press censorship was imposed on the 24th and thereafter one can find very little on local military activities in the Vancouver newspapers.

It appears that the federal government had no intention of endowing Vancouver with permanent defences and that the gun batteries established in 1914 were only a stop-gap measure to be removed once British naval superiority was achieved in the Pacific Ocean. Fear that this might be the case was expressed in a resolution introduced by Mr. H.O. Bell-Irving and unanimously passed by the Vancouver Board of Trade of September 8th. The Board commended the government for "placing guns in Stanley Park and at Point Grey, and recognizing the importance to the whole Dominion of the adequate defence of the port of Vancouver,..." It "respectfully" urged "That the batteries be completed and (fully) manned at the earliest moment possible" and that part of the naval reserve be stationed in the city.[16]

The Point Grey battery was the first to go. Canada gave most of her 60-pounder guns and other stores to the British army and by the end of September the Cobourg Heavy Battery was back in Ontario. It is probable, but not certain, that the artillery section of the Home Guard reverted to infantry and, when the German threat to the Pacific coast disappeared, that it disbanded. The Stanley Park guns were, by June 1915, neither manned nor operational. It is not known if they were ever used by the militia artillery.

The men of the Lower Mainland who wanted to serve with the artillery of the Canadian Expeditionary Force in Europe were enrolled in the 68th Overseas Depot Battery, raised in March 1916; the 15th Brigade, Canadian Field Artillery, whose headquarters were mobilized at Vancouver in April 1916; and the 85th Battery, C.F.A. The 85th Battery, which was authorized in July 1918, spent six months at Vladivostok as part of the Canadian Siberian Expeditionary Force supporting the White Russians against the Bolsheviks. Unlike the Canadian gunners in Western Russia, these men did not see action and they were withdrawn in April 1919. Many others served in Flanders and France as individuals with other artillery formations.

The dispatch of recruits for overseas service and the abandonment of the two protective batteries reflected the confidence in the security of the west coast after 1914. The strong allied fleet assembled in September kept von Spee's squadron from moving north of Central America. The blockade of Tsingtao cut the squadron off from its home base and it was denied havens in its customary area of operations by the capture of Germany's Pacific Ocean colonies. Von Spee was now dependent on chance captures and the goodwill of neutral states for coal and food. One cruiser was detached for raiding in the Indian Ocean and the remainder of the squadron steamed southward along the coast of Chile. On November 1st, 1914, a pursuing British squadron caught up with the German warships off Cape Coronel. Hidden by the outline of the shore and with the aid of superior gunnery, the Germans destroyed their pursuers. Four Canadian midshipmen were on board one of the ill-fated ships of the Royal Navy. A stronger fleet under Admiral Sturdee awaited von Spee's squadron at the Falkland Islands and when the German warships passed the Horn to enter the South Atlantic they were caught on December 8th. **Leipzig** and **Nurnberg** were sunk and von Spee went down with his flagship. Only the swift **Dresden** escaped to live for three more months before she too was cornered and sunk.

CHAPTER 4

Marking Time Between the Wars

The fury of World War One was still very much alive when in January 1918 Major General Sir William Otter recommended to the Minister of Militia that the impending demobilization of Canadian Expeditionary Force units would afford "an unparalleled opportunity for the reorganization and territorial readjustments of Units of the Active Militia".[1] With cessation of hostilities on November 11th, 1918 and the dust of battle hardly settled, there came a flood of requests to the Militia Minister petitioning him to perpetuate in the post-war Militia many of those C.E.F. Units which had distinguished themselves during four years of war. Vancouver was just one of the many communities which hoped for the establishment of an artillery unit of its own. In the spring of 1919 a "Committee of Militia Reorganization," better known as the Otter Committee, was established with General Otter as president. From September to December the committee visited every Military District in Canada listening to many proposals for the inclusion of units from all branches of the C.E.F.

In the first half of 1919 almost every train brought a steady stream of men for discharge. It was not long before men who had lived and fought together sought to continue their comradeship by forming associations. One such group was the "Vancouver Overseas Artillery Association", which after a short time of sharing space with another association decided to leave and joined a group of Engineers to form "The Gunners and Sappers".[2] This club served a most useful purpose in keeping together a nucleus of officers and non-commissioned officers with a wealth of artillery experience. At the request of the Otter Committee a group of eleven returned artillery officers, five of whom would become future Brigade Commanding Officers, met on December 16th 1919, in the officers' mess of the Drill Hall on Cambie Street to discuss the organization of the Militia Artillery in Vancouver. Some of the motions passed at this meeting had rather rich expectations.

That inasmuch, the success, efficiency, and esprit de corps of the Brigade lies in fostering the social side and corporate life of the Unit, it is recommended that the accommodation provided be such that would permit of this necessary development, and should include:

One Large Room for each Battery, that could be used for instruction, lectures, dances, smoking, concerts, etc.,
Bowling Alley
Swimming Bath
Gymnasium
Club Rooms   )
Canteen   ) all comfortably furnished[3]
Officers' mess)

As there was no existing artillery drill hall a motion was put forth that Lieut. R.T. Perry be requested to design an ideal drill hall. The actual armoury constructed would be far from ideal, and would be thirteen years in coming, but the architect was Lieutenant Perry who was by that time Commanding Officer of the Brigade. Horses were one of the attractions of the artillery and the efficiency of the Brigade hinged largely on its standard of equitation, and so it was moved that there should be "ten riders, thirty-six light draft" horses on the permanent establishment of the Brigade. This would allow sufficient mounts for riding practice, drills and week-end exercises. The meeting also recommended the attachment of a permanent staff of an Adjutant, Regimental Sergeant Major, Regimental Quartermaster Seargeant, Brigade Artificer, and clerk. That took fifty years to achieve! A change in uniform colour to blue was recommended as it would make a smarter uniform and because the "men were tired of Khaki". While some of the motions may have seemed frivolous, one was to have a profound effect on the success of the Brigade in the future.[4]

That inasmuch as, such a policy will attract a better class of recruits and ensure a nucleus of highly trained men, that would be extremely useful in the event of mobilization, this meeting recommend that training should be of a continuous character and of a nature that would develop efficient up-to-date Artillery men and not merely gun numbers; and that the scientific side of Artillery work should be given prominence, and the subject of Artillery cooperation with other branches should be thoroughly instructed.

In a letter to the Vancouver Association in January of 1920, Brigadier General A.G.L. McNaughton informed them that guns for a Brigade were now on their way from England. He took the opportunity to pass on the appreciation of the Deputy Inspector General of Artillery for their assistance in preparing for the Re-Organization Scheme and their active assistance in making the re-organization an accomplished fact.[5] The Department of Militia acted quickly on the Otter Committee recommendations, one of which was formation of a Field Artillery Brigade in Vancouver to be known as the 15th Brigade, Canadian Field Artillery. It was authorized on February 2nd, 1920 with the following organization:[6]

Headquarters Vancouver; organized July 15th, 1920
31st Battery CFA-Vancouver; organized July 15th, 1920
68th Battery CFA-North Vancouver; organized July 15th, 1920 and relocalized at Vancouver on March 1st, 1922
85th Battery CFA-New Westminster; organized July 15th, 1920 and relocalized at Vancouver on March 1st, 1922
Ammunition Column-Vancouver; organized January 15th, 1921
Attached: 5th Siege Battery CA-Vancouver; organized July 15th, 1920
Detached: 58th Battery CFA-Victoria; attached to 5th (British Columbia) Regiment Canadian Garrison Artillery; organized September 22nd, 1920

Lieutenant F.T. Coghlan DSO, an experienced artillery officer who had commanded the 9th and 11th Field Brigade in France, was the first commanding officer of the Brigade.

The Brigade's first home was not quite what the "fathers of the Brigade" had visualized because the unit moved into the Horse Show Building on West Georgia Street near the entrance to Stanley Park. A future commanding officer made this comment about the building:[7]

> It has the advantage of a riding ring and stopped at that. Damply hot in summer, misty and leaky in winter, filled with gloomy rows of dusty, unsafe galleries, reeking first of horse manure and later of Carbolic Acid, it was our home for twelve years. We worked in it, we played in it, and we grew to regard it with that strong affection which made the Belgian Peasantry cling to their hovels under shell fire.

Twelve years were to pass before a permanent home was to be a reality. Had a 1924 recommendation of Prime Minister Mackenzie-King been implemented, it might never have even reached the drawing board. King called for at least one hundred armouries and drill halls to be converted to community halls, "a transition from military to community purposes", he said, that would be, "much in accord with the spirit of our time".[8]

As a result of Government demands for restraint in spending - a phrase all too familiar to the Militia during the next decade and a half - there would be no funds in 1920 for a summer camp. Recruiting, organizing batteries and a "happy go lucky sort of training" were to carry through to the spring of 1921. Hastings Park (the present Pacific National Exhibition Ground) was to be the site of the Brigade's first summer camp in July 1921. Whenever guns and ammunition limbers were to be moved horses had to be rented, as the Brigade was never to receive a permanent establishment of horses. Horses for this first move were to come from a local knacker (a trader in horses fit only for animal food) who had recently received a shipment of "meat" from the Prairies. Somehow by 0800 hours these nags were to be transformed into six-horse hitches to pull the guns to Hastings Park. The officers, accustomed to the smooth working of seasoned men and horses, found it necessary to turn the clock back as they wrestled with the problems of the one night a week soldier. The move did not take place until 1100 hours and only then with the aid of much bad language. The men were unused to the horses and the horses unused to men. "Granville Street was crossed at noon amidst an awe-struck populace"[9] and by late afternoon the first gun and wagon arrived at the Park. Training was described as "cheerful and willing, rather than well-informed"[10] as the men groomed their steeds to the best of their knowledge and then quickly asked for leave to ride on the nearby roller-coaster. By the week's end the drill and discipline had advanced considerably and the move home was in infinitely better style. Later in August the first live firing camp was held at Sarcee, on the outskirts of Calgary, Alberta. This camp was to become a familiar one to many gunners over the next decade. With the duties of the day completed, a visit to Calgary was in order. Prohibition was in effect in Alberta, so to quench one's thirst it was the custom:[11]

> To call upon a gentleman, who maintained the outward appearance of a drug store by a visible display of tooth brushes, - this was in front, business being done in the rear only. Reaching up between two bottles labelled "Cyanide of Potassium" he would pour out a Homoepathic drachm at a charge warranted neither by the quantity nor quality, and at least make one glad of his escape. It was harder to obtain beer. You had to join a club - in this manner: From the street you walked into an old fashioned brass-railed affair, where the lad-in-the-white-apron would serve some fearful compound known unto the Law as Foamo or Prairie Fluid. Moved by the look of agony on one's face he would indicate the-little-door-to-the-side. This was the club, but the rules were strict - you had to sign a book agreeing to uphold the constitution.

It was a very hot summer and the pace of training was slow. Batteries were low in numbers and only very simple firing practices were carried out. This was in contrast to future camps when units vied for the many trophies sponsored by the Canadian Artillery Association.

The Brigade was armed with the 18-pounder gun for the field batteries and the 60-pounder for the 5th Siege Battery. Gun drill and riding took on a more serious outlook following the first camps, and when it came time for the 1922 camp a far different Brigade arrived in Sarcee. Local winter training at the Horse Show Building had been interspersed with indoor baseball for the men and polo for the officers. The first honours to fall upon the Brigade were most impressive when at the 1922 camp the 31st Battery won the Governor General's and Earl of Stradbrook Cups for general efficiency, the Grant Challenge Cup for tactics, the Macdonald Challenge Trophy for gun laying and signalling and the Hurdman Challenge Cup plus a cash prize of $140 for the efficiency of personnel competition, a record unequalled in the history of the Artillery Association Competitions![12] The Battery went on to win three of these cups again in 1923. At considerable expense the 60-pounders would be loaded on Canadian Pacific Rail flatcars and taken to camp. A year or two later one gun was taken all the way to Sarcee for the sole purpose of asking one officer three questions on equipment as part of his qualifying exam. After that, expense dictated an end to hauling the guns over the Rockies. There would be no firing camp in 1924 as the Government again withheld funds from the Militia. On July 1st, 1925 the Brigade became known as the 15th Field Brigade Canadian Artillery and its attached battery became the 5th Medium Battery.

By the late 1920's many armies were experimenting with the mechanization of their artillery and in Canada the 5th Medium Battery was to be one of the leaders in this field. The Permanent Force had carried out some mechanical transport trials using six-wheeled vehicles to tow 18-pounders at Ottawa in May 1928. The training exercise under the command of Major J.G. Chutter, MC on the week-end of June 9th, 1928 must have been a first for the Non Permanent Artillery. Excerpts from Major Chutter's report relate some facts of this experiment.[13]

> On Thursday evening we practised the hitching of 18 pdr. guns to motor trucks, so that on Saturday afternoon there should be no delay. We left the Horse Show building, our Armoury, at 3 o'clock, Saturday afternoon, 38 all ranks, 4 18-pdr. guns, 4 International trucks and 5 motor cars.
>
> Before going any further I should mention that I had told the Battery Captain that we were going out for approximately 30 hours with approximately 40 men and that we should bivouac for the night; that I wanted him to make arrangements for the feeding and comfort of the Battery and that he had at his disposal 65¢ per man.
>
> Our passage through the streets of Vancouver caused no little comment, as it was the first time for 7 years that a Battery had passed through the City, the last time being the moving of the Brigade from the Horse Show building to Hastings Park in 1921 for training purposes.
>
> After travelling for about 20 minutes we halted to examine the equipment and found that minor adjustments had to be made in ropes between trucks and guns - generally speaking these were working very satisfactorily, we subsequently found that a speed of 10 miles an hour could be maintained on pavement, and 7 on rough country roads, without causing too much vibration to the guns.
>
> The truck drivers, who were all ex-service men, entered into the spirit of the work, and did things with the trucks, such as crossing small ditches and running into fields, which were little short of marvellous.

Contrast a day so spent with one on horses. Approximately three times the amount of training was accomplished and very much more ground covered, besides it proved interesting, not too fatiguing for the detachments and very much less expensive.

The week-end was brought to a very happy conclusion on the terrace of Shannon, where Mrs. B.T. Rogers entertained the Battery to afternoon tea.

Patience, foresight and dedication finally won out over an apathetic public and opposition in Parliament. The **Vancouver Daily Province** headline of July 28th, 1931 announced, "Drill Hall Will Be Constructed In Kitsilano". To hide the cost of new armoury construction a private organization would plan and build the structure and then have the government lease it and later take ownership. This, in a nutshell, was the plan proposed in August 1928 when the Vancouver Armoury Association Limited was formed. The objects for which the company was established were, "to erect and construct an Armoury and Drill Hall in the area known as Greater Vancouver, to purchase, lease, take in exchange or otherwise acquire lands...to sell, lease, exchange, or otherwise dispose of to His Majesty the King...any of the buildings or structures erected thereon".[14] The founders were W.A. Townsley (Commanding Officer), J.G. Chutter (Battery Commander), R.T. Perry (Architect and future Commanding Officer), C.G. Beeston (future Commanding Officer), H.R. Bray (Brigade Officer), and Brigadier General Victor Odlum. W.C. Woodward of Woodward Stores, Honorary Lieutenant Colonel of the Brigade, later became a director of the Armouries Association. Property was purchased on West 11th Avenue and construction began in September, 1932. Moving day for the 15th Brigade and the British Columbia Hussars, with whom they shared quarters, came early in 1933 after a thirteen year wait. The new facility was not quite as splendid as the Brigade "fathers" had hoped for, but it was comfortable and functional. At a mess dinner of the Brigade officers in the Hotel Georgia the District Commander announced that the Governor General had granted permission to use his name for the Armoury.[15] The Earl of Bessborough officially opened the Armoury on March 27th, 1934.[15] The Seaforth Highlanders also used a private organization, formed in 1931, to construct their armouries on Burrard Street. Such measures were forced on the supporters of the militia by a tight-fisted government and the Great Depression.

Events in the Far East were to have a direct effect on the Brigade, which in June of 1935 changed its title to the 15th Field Brigade, Royal Canadian Artillery. Japan's move into Manchuria and her naval build up sparked considerable debate on our ability to defend the West Coast. Writing about the defence of the West Coast, Prof. A.R.M. Lower suggested that Canadians had little consciousness of coasts, and vaguely supposed that vast expanses of sea and either the Royal Navy or the United States Navy would protect us. He felt that West-Coasters "still think of the sea as merely a place to bathe in".[17] This view was expressed in an address to Vancouver Kinsmen when Brigadier General V.W. Odlum said of the Japanese threat, "We are wonderfully protected by the Pacific and Vancouver Island and no military force would think of attacking us". Nonetheless public feeling in general was that something must be done to bolster the meagre defences. In a rousing address by Colonel H.F.G. Letson to the Vancouver Board of Trade in April 1938 he bared the problem of B.C. defences and the plight of the militiaman who carries on despite public apathy, lack of boots, ill-fitting shoddy uniforms, lack of pay and the loss of either his pay or his job should he attend annual training camp. He reported hearing responsible men say, "He is a good lad but he would go further if he did not waste his time on the Militia".[18]

The Department of National Defence finally faced the weak position of the Pacific defences. Major B.C.D. Treatt, Royal Artillery, from the Coast Artillery School, Shoeburyness, England, was engaged to survey and report upon existing and potential coast defence sites. Following his visit in October of 1936, Major Treatt recommended a number of new sites and the improvement of some existing ones, thus adding a little flesh to the skeleton defences. His thorough report was endorsed in the main by the Joint Staff Committee and early in 1937 Parliament approved the construction of a number of new sites. Four were directly related to the defence of the Port of Vancouver: Ferguson Point (Stanley Park), Point Grey, First Narrows (North side), and Yorke Island, about 150 miles northwest of Vancouver off the eastern coast of Vancouver Island. In planning the armament necessary for these installations the Joint Staff Committee had drawn up a "Form and Scale of Attack" based on the premise that "the British Empire is at war (USA neutral) with Japan".[19] The forms of attack likely to be mounted against Vancouver and Yorke Island were: firstly, an attack by one armed merchant vessel with 6-inch guns to bombard the port or lay mines in the harbour approaches; secondly, an attack by up to four motor torpedo boats; and thirdly, an attack by up to two submarines armed with 4.7-inch guns to attack the port at close range by gunfire and lay mines or torpedo ships in the harbour. To meet these possible attacks a counter bombardment and close defence battery of three 6-inch guns would be built at Point Grey. Counter bombardment refers to guns capable of engaging bombarding vessels, and close defence refers to batteries designed to repel closer range attacks by destroyers, submarines and motor boats. A two gun 6-inch close defence battery at Ferguson Point and an Anti Motor Torpedo Boat Battery of two 12-pounders and one 6-pounder duplex at First Narrows would complete the plan. Approximately ten Coast Artillery Searchlights would support the guns. They were to be employed in detecting vessels, illuminating targets for the 6-inch guns and providing an illuminated area for the 12-pounders at First Narrows. An interesting point of detail in the planning was the concern about a possible torpedo attack on the piers of the planned Lions Gate bridge at the First Narrows. Recommendations were made to ask the Department of Public Works to ensure that specifications for the piers would include gun platforms for the AMTB guns. Plans also called for torpedo nets or obstructions which would cause torpedos to explode a safe distance from the bridge piers.[20] These recommendations were not acted upon. Preparation of the first site at Ferguson Point began in February, 1938 with The Vancouver Town Planning Commission to be the battery's first attacker. The encounter is recorded under the **Daily Province** banner "Beauty Takes the Count", as the City Council decided against supporting the objections of the commission. The Commission had hoped that the Department of National Defense might find a location other than Ferguson Point, on the grounds that "the selected location was a favourite beauty spot in the park" and that local authorities such as the Parks Board and City Council should be consulted in selecting the gun positions.[21]

By now both defence plan announcements and rumours of change were frequent. The 15th Brigade carried on and attended annual camp in July 1937 at Shilo, Manitoba, unaware that this was their last opportunity until 1948 to experience the excitement and mobility of field guns on the move. The bad news, perhaps inevitable, was disclosed early in 1938 when all officers were called into the Officers' Mess. Brigadier J.C. Stewart, the District Commander, announced that the Brigade would assume a coast defence role and would be responsible for manning the Vancouver Defences. Some were to resent this change that condemned them to be "concrete gunners sitting on their fannies looking at the water". On April 7th, 1938, the Brigade, with four batteries and one attached, became the 15th Coast Brigade R.C.A.; the designation "Vancouver" was added in July. The changeover came just in time for the Brigade to prepare for its first Coast Defence Camp held in July at Fort Macaulay, Esquimalt. Officers and men were enthusiastic as they fired targets towed by H.M.C.S. **Armentieres** and "fountains of water churned by bursting shells provided an exciting spectacle as the Vancouver artillerymen, though new to the guns, surprised their Permanent Force instructors with their accuracy".[22] While awaiting completion of the Stanley Park Battery, the men practised gun drill at Vancouver with a mock gun made out of a telephone pole.

Provision of coast artillery was a start. But now many were asking, where is the air defence for the city? The **Daily Province** posed this question in its editorial of May 31st, 1938.[23]

What preparation have we for such a contingency? Sending out Khaki uniforms and rifles for the boys (unemployed on relief) in the Post Office, doss house and the tin-canners in Oakalla will avail nothing. They would be as helpless against a modern bomber as the two six-inch guns in Stanley Park.

No hostile power would be so foolish as to force the Straits of Juan de Fuca in order to engage the Stanley Park battery, when it could send a sub carrying a bomber into one of the Vancouver Island west coast inlets, or let loose a squadron from a mother ship off the coast, to fly to Vancouver in an hour or so. Where is there an anti-aircraft battery on the Pacific Coast?[22]

Action began a year later when formation of the 1st Anti-Aircraft Regiment R.C.A. was announced in May 1939. The 68th Battery and the 15th Brigade's attached 5th Battery provided the initial manpower and became the 9th and 11th Batteries of the new regiment. The commanding officer of the 15th Brigade, Lt. Col. G.Y.L. Crossley, stated, "I am glad to hear that the department is now able to implement what it has long recognized as a pressing need for the defense of Vancouver", that the "formation of the anti-aircraft unit has been only delayed because it was not possible to get the guns in the past".[24] Little did he know that events shaping in Europe would delay the arrival of the first anti-aircraft gun for three years.

The need for personnel to man the searchlights which were to be used in conjunction with the coast artillery necessitated a new organization. This was solved by disbanding the British Columbia Hussars (Armoured Car) to create the 1st Searchlight Regiment R.C.A. in May, 1939. Although the Hussars were designated armoured car, their vehicles consisted of motorcycles with sidecars and Morris sports cars - hardly armoured! As with the 1st Anti-Aircraft, equipment would be a long two and a half years in arriving. This was the only searchlight regiment formed in Canada; elsewhere only units of battery size were formed.

Although the Brigade was now coast artillery, it did manage to retain the beloved 18-pounder for the purpose of firing artillery salutes on such occasions as Dominion Day, the King's Birthday, and visits of the Governor General. Salutes were usually fired from a point near the Nine O'clock Gun in Stanley Park. War clouds continued to gather in Europe as the Brigade sailed for what was to be its last peacetime camp at Esquimalt in July, 1939. Few were to dream that August would see many of them practising their newly learned skills in the forts of Vancouver and Yorke Island.

CHAPTER 5

Take Post!

For the gunners of Vancouver the Second World War began fifteen days before Canada's declaration of war against Germany. The Allies' reaction to Nazi aggression against Poland had been anticipated. On August 25th Ottawa ordered the mobilization of three Vancouver militia units, including the 15th Coast Brigade. The callup for the 1st Searchlight Regiment (formerly the B.C. Hussars) soon followed. From Victoria the 5th (B.C.) Coast Brigade, Royal Canadian Artillery, went out to man the coastal forts at Esquimalt and Albert Head. "The militia will cover vulnerable points throughout the province as part of a pre-arranged programme of defence" said Brigadier J.C. Stewart, commander of the military district.[1] The men were still free to choose whether or not to accept fulltime service with the army. "This army is becoming too bloody dangerous" quipped an officer as the gunners assembled at the Bessborough Armouries to volunteer and to be assigned their duties. A detachment, the 85th Heavy Battery, sailed for Yorke Island on the night of the 29th. The 31st Battery of the brigade took charge of the nearly-complete battery in Stanley Park and six men were detached to occupy the north side of the First Narrows. Pending the completion of huts on Point Grey, the 58th Battery was quartered in the armouries.

R. Theo DuMoulin, then commander of the 58th Battery, remembered the rainy weekend when the brigade was mobilized and work began on the "fort" at Point Grey. Men of the Royal Canadian Engineers laboured at night under flood lamps banging together huts while buildings of the Dominion Wireless Station provided temporary shelter for meals. On September 3rd the entire battery took up quarters on the sandy headland overlooking the Strait of Georgia. Two 6-inch calibre coastal guns were delivered to the site by barge. The elaborate concrete emplacements for which they were destined did not yet exist and temporary positions were built on top of the cliffs. Quick-drying cement, rushed in from Seattle, was used to lay down supporting aprons for the pivot mountings of the guns. Around these were built two-tiered wooden platforms reinforced with sandbags and backfill. Cupboards for shells and charges were built into the rear of the platforms. The cordite they contained, however, is an unstable explosive that requires a controlled temperature and a dry atmosphere. T. Murray Hunter, who was a second lieutenant of the 58th Battery, had "a clear recollection, from those hectic days of August 1939, of rows of 6-inch projectiles standing under tarpaulins in the driving rain."[2] Twenty yards behind the guns was a small wooden command post on stilts while a battery observation post was built on a point of land two hundred and fifty yards to the left of the emplacements. For a year the gunners used these makeshift structures while to the rear three reinforced concrete emplacements with attached crew shelters were constructed. Each new position had its own underground magazines linked together by a tunnel that also provided access to a new concrete battery command post. The magazines were protected from enemy gunfire by a blanket of earth and one yard thick concrete "busters" to explode any shell that penetrated the ground.

Construction of the Narrows North fort proceeded at a faster pace. Two 12-pounder guns had been provisionally located on a gravel spit at the mouth of the Capilano River. On October 6th, 1939 they were moved to the roof of the three storey, concrete "gantry" beneath Lions' Gate Bridge. It was not a moment too soon since two weeks later heavy rains flooded the old gunsites and half of the camp. To assist the guns at night, eight manually-controlled, 18-inch reflector searchlights were installed on the north shore. It was said that some of the searchlights had come from Niagara Falls where they had illuminated the cascade for honeymooners. They were used in a similar fashion by the gunners of Narrows North who illuminated the ferry to Victoria as it carried away a newlywed comrade. It was also a favourite trick of the soldiers to flick the beams onto Prospect Point after midnight and, with the aid of binoculars, watch surprised lovers disentangle themselves to escape the all-revealing glare. In February and March 1941 the smaller searchlights were replaced by three 60-inch diameter, dispersed-beam searchlights. At 800,000,000 candlepower apiece, these modern lights were one hundred times more powerful than their predecessors and they could penetrate the darkness for a distance of three to five miles. These powerful beacons were located in what, to the casual observer, appeared to be boat huts. The fronts dropped down when the beams were to light up the narrows.

By December 1941 there were ten large, carbon-arc searchlights whose beams swept the entrance of Burrard Inlet. Classified as either fighting (concentrated beam) or observation (dispersed beam) defence electric lights, the searchlights were usually housed in concrete or wooden structures on the flanks of the gun batteries. They were placed close to the water level so that their beams would shine across the surface to reveal any object, as small as a periscope, sticking out of the water. Before the arrival of the new searchlights, drifting logs and canoes had caused a number of false alarms.

The full extent of the Vancouver coastal defences and their role in the protection of Canada's west coast were outlined in the local Fire Commander's Orders of October 1942. In keeping with security regulations, the earlier standing orders issued by the commanding officer, who was customarily the Fire Commander, had been destroyed and the 1942 orders are the oldest ones in existence. The standing orders reveal that though the defences were elaborate they were also deficient in many things.

1. *Role of the Fortress in the Scheme of Defence.*
   The extreme outer defences of British Columbia are supplied by the R.C.N. patrol vessels and R.C.A.F. seaplane patrols. Owing to the prevalence of fog in the summer and South-Easterly gales with rain and snow in the winter off the West Coast, it is pos-

sible for an enemy to elude observation, in which case he would meet the forts in the Straits of Juan de Fuca, Yorke Island or Prince Rupert.

For the defence of Vancouver, the Forts on both sides of the Straits of Juan de Fuca and the Fort at Yorke Island act as barriers to an attack on Vancouver. There is considerable amount of fog in the Straits of Juan de Fuca and Naval Authorities advise it is quite impossible for a determined enemy to slip past Victoria in fog or at night, to attack Vancouver.

The Fort at Yorke Island guarding Johnston Straits is equipped with two 6" Mk VII guns with a limited range of about 11,000 yards, consequently it is quite possible for an enemy to force his way past these defences on the way to Vancouver or Bremerton, by water.

The role of the Forts in Vancouver is to repel any hostile vessel in the waters adjacent and to assist in repelling any troops attempting to land on shore. For this purpose, the Forts are allotted as follows:

Point Grey: Designed for a counter-bombardment battery of three 6" B.L. (breech-loading) guns on 45° mountings. Owing to the difficulties in obtaining 45° mountings from England, they are mounted on 15° mountings, consequently are only adapted for close defence.

Stanley Park: Close defence battery guarding English Bay and the First Narrows entrance to Burrard Inlet, equipped with two 4.7" B.L. guns on 20° mountings.

Narrows North: Two 12-pdr. guns. Close defence against Destroyers, M.T.B.'s (motor torpedo boats) or small craft.

Steveston: Two 18-pdr. Q.F. (quick-firing) Field guns to guard the South arm of the Fraser River and to prevent vessels proceeding up the South Arm to New Westminster.

Point Atkinson: One 18-pdr. Q.F. Field gun - very limited use in defence.

Examination Batteries (to challenge and detain incoming ships): Point Grey and Point Atkinson.

As the arc of fire of Point Grey does not cover the Examination Anchorage (in English Bay), Stanley Park is responsible for covering any vessels in the Examination Anchorage.(...)

5. Defensive Measures Against Air Attack. (...)
   (e) Defence - The R.C.A.F. has fighter squadrons and is responsible to employ them to the best advantage in Air Raid defence - but - all Forts are responsible for their own local defence.
   (f) Active Defence - Bren guns and rifles supplied for defence (against) land attack have to be sited so that they can be used for defence against air attack. (...) The Bren guns supplied are equipped with A.A. (anti-aircraft) mountings and are sited so that they can be used for Air Defence. (...)
   (g) P.A.D. (passive air defence) - Point Grey and Stanley Park are equipped with slit trenches, but owing to the nature of the ground at Narrows North and Steveston, sandbag protection is all that is available. The tunnels and magazines at Stanley Park and Point Grey are also available for use as Air Raid shelters in times of emergency. (...)

COMMUNICATIONS

1. TELEPHONE.
   (a) Command Line - A line used for tactical purposes only is carried over B.C. Tele-

phone Lines, which is bridged through their exchange for perpetual hook-up, with an Exchange at the F.C. (fire command) Post.

Code Names.

Fire Command Post ———————————— F.C.
Point Atkinson ———————————— ZA
Narrows North ———————————— ZB
Stanley Park ———————————— ZC
Point Grey ———————————— ZD

B.O.P. (battery observation post) Point Grey Naval Control Office, Marine Building.

B. Steveston Battery is not included on this line.

(b) *Submarine Cable - A 2-way submarine cable exists between Point Grey and Point Atkinson for the purpose of communication between the Examination Battery (Point Grey) and P.W.S.S. [port war signal station] (Point Atkinson).*

The forts could also communicate with one another and the examination vessels by radio and the entire Vancouver defence system was linked by the telephone system. In addition to the battery code names, there was a code for the alert states of the fire command. Beginning with "Sword" and working up through "Scabbard" and "Spear" the code reached "Dagger" which meant assume battle stations.

Taken literally, the Fire Commander's Orders of October 1942 could be misleading. The "patrol vessels" of the Royal Canadian Navy then consisted of three minesweepers and a few auxiliary vessels supplemented by the boats of the Fishermen's Reserve. The four destroyers formerly stationed at Esquimalt had been transferred to the Atlantic coast. The Royal Canadian Air Force "seaplane patrols" originated largely from the Jericho Beach Air Station on English Bay. This pioneer air station had been established on a part of the old naval reserve in 1920 and during the Second World War it was a base for the double-winged Blackburn Sharks and Supermarine Stranraers.[4] It was the two-engined Stranraer that patrolled the length of British Columbia's coastline and sent back radio reports on all ships sighted. A brace of twenty-pound bombs hung below each wing. The Vancouver defences also had the support of a squadron of aircraft based at the Patricia Bay airfield.

The Victoria-Esquimalt batteries covering the Juan de Fuca strait were indeed formidable and they were coordinated with guns on the American side. There was a 9.2-inch calibre battery at Albert Head, two 6-inch batteries and four positions armed with 12-pounders. The guns were as old and their mountings as deficient as those at Vancouver. Yorke Island to the north had been bolstered by exchanging its original 4.7-inch guns for the 6-inch pieces at Stanley Park. The exchange was accomplished in the summer of 1942 in what was supposed to be secrecy. The security achieved may be judged from the fact that a gunner on Yorke Island received a letter from his wife in Vancouver reporting the arrival of the 4.7-inch guns.

Canada traditionally depended on Britain for heavy armaments but in wartime whatever could be produced was devoted to home defence. When shipments of arms to Canada resumed it was the Atlantic coast that received priority. War with Japan came fifteen months after mobilization and the threat from the Orient seemed less immediate than the danger posed by German submarines on the east coast. This meant that the coastal batteries of British Columbia used weapons that were already on hand in Canada and, when coastal guns were not available, they employed First World War field guns. The coastal artillery was of Boer War vintage and the sights and mountings were deficient. The prob-

Jericho Beach Air Station in September 1941 with a Supermarine Stranraer flying boat (Below); these aircraft patrolled the coastal waters of British Columbia in wartime.

Credit: Public Archives of Canada, National Photography Collection.

The construction of the temporary emplacements for the two 6-inch calibre guns at Point Grey in September 1939.
Credit: Department of National Defence.

Point Grey Fort in September 1941 with the University of British Columbia campus in the background: the three gun emplacements can be seen in the clearing at the cliff top with the camp behind; the searchlight towers on the beach are lost in the shadows.
Credit: Public Archives of Canada, National Photography Collection.

The temporary command post (upper left) and flank observation post built at Point Grey in 1939. From this O.P. Peter Stursberg watched a practice shoot in February 1940. In the lower left, an observer trains binoculars on Georgia Strait with a telephone and alarm bells behind him. Centre top shows the depression range finder in the same location which established the range and bearing of a ship.

Credit: Department of National Defence.

The permanent gun emplacements and command post at Point Grey in May 1943: steel wool camouflage had just been installed over wood and metal frameworks to conceal the battery from air observation. (Below Left), a gun crew on No. 1 gun drives home a shell into the bore of the weapon.

Credit: Department of National Defence.

67

Point Atkinson in April 1943: the large buildings in the centre are the lighthouse keeper's residence and the hut for the naval personnel who manned the signals station next to the lighthouse. (Below) the beacon and connected to it by a catwalk are the wooden engine room and the smaller gun shed which housed the 18-pounder examination gun. The gunners who served these installations and the flanking searchlights were quartered in a camp at the end of the narrow gauge railway running north from the wharf.
Credit: Public Archives of Canada, National Photography Collection.

"Little Alcatraz" in May 1942: Yorke Island in Johnstone Strait seen from the west with the mainland in the background. The guns were in the clearing on the left; the wharf appears in the lower right, and the searchlight emplacements can be seen along the shoreline.
Credit: Major R.V. Stevenson.

Life on Yorke Island in 1939-40: (Top, left to right) Dick Jenkins, Denny Mackie and Pat sail north on the <u>Lady Rose.</u> Seen from a wharf littered with building materials is the oldest building on the island which became the officers' quarters. (Centre) Huts for the other ranks had to be built; in this case the work is done Tarzan-style. Bud Garrett and Ken Foote are taking their ease in the Mary

Helen; boating and fishing with grenades provided diversion. (Bottom) Sheltering from the prevailing wind in the rocks, Harry Mumford, Dick Jenkins and Len Cuddeford write letters to home. With heads shaven, boys of the Canadian Scottish Company on the island masquerade as "enemy" captives of a Canadian soldier who wears a wash basin for a helmet.

Credit: P.R. Jenkins.

Yorke Island in 1943: (Above), men of the Royal Canadian Engineers work on a roadway behind the battery observation post and gun emplacements. (Below), stores are unloaded at the wharf from the supply boat on the far side; the water scow and examination boat are moored on the left.

Yorke Island in 1943: Orville N. Fisher, a war artist, visited the battery observation post and drew pictures of a gunner taking a sighting through a Mark V Depression Range Finder.

Credit:
Canadian War Museum,
National Museum of Man,
National Museums of Canada.

The Coastal Guns: (Above) A 6-inch Mark VII, Breech-Loading gun at Yorke Island overlooks Johnstone Strait. (Below) At the Stanley Park battery a 4.7-inch Mark IV, Quick-firing gun is loaded and then elevated for firing. These drawings were made in March 1943 by Orville N. Fisher after the guns had been exchanged between the two locations.

Two signallers on duty.

Canadian War Museum, National Museum of Man, National Museums of Canada.

Events in the life of a Coastal Gunner: (Right) The funeral of Bdr. Bajus passes down Georgia St. on September 16th, 1939 (Far right) Dressed in summer kit, the Narrows North detachment goes on a route march up Capilano Canyon in 1940. Bottom (From left to right) A corporal's guard in greatcoats and armed with Ross rifles poses outside the Bessborough Armouries. A woodcutting party under Sgt. Mangles clears trees from the line of fire of No. 3 Gun at Point Grey in 1944. The first Victory Loan parade at Alert Bay featured a detachment from Yorke Island.

Credit: Harry Mangles and Jim Saddler.

The Examination Service: The H.M.C.S. <u>Allaverdy</u>, manned by men of the navy and the Fishermen's Reserve, was one of the examination vessels. (Top Right) is a 6-pounder Hotchkiss gun at Point Grey that fired warning shots ahead of vessels that ignored security rules. The signaller at Yorke Island was communicating with a ship by means of an aldis lamp.

Credit:
B.C. Provincial Archives, Jim Saddler, Canadian War Museum. National Museum of Man, National Museums of Canada.

The Coastal Guns in Action: (Top, left to right) "Gunners Want to See Action" read the caption for this 1940 press photo that looks down the muzzle of a 6-inch gun at Point Grey. The men in the pit are operating the traversing mechanism on the pivot mounting; this was later done electrically. A picture of a 4.7-inch gun on Yorke Island taken in the autumn of 1939; these positions and those at Stanley Park were later given concrete and steel overhead cover to protect the gunners from shrapnel. (Below) The camouflaged guns at Point Grey in 1943; they were nearly invisible from seaward. Night firing of a 6-inch gun at Mary Hill on Vancouver Island.

Credit: P.N. Moogk, Harry Mangles, Canadian War Museum, National Museum of Man, National Museums of Canada and Fort Rodd Hill National Historic Park.

Searchlight Emplacements: (Top, Left to Right) The positions at r rows North resembled boat huts. One of the two emplacement Yorke Island is shown with its shutters closed and an armed ser on duty. (Below), a gunner at Siwash Rock adjusts the turning ap ratus on a 60-inch diameter light. The searchlights at Point G were in towers that were painted to blend into the bank behi

Credit: Fort Rodd Hill National Historic Park, P.R. Jenkins, and the Canadian War Muse

75

Point Grey Fort in 1943-44: (Top, left to right) The Battery Observation Post is shown without camouflage. Inside, on the second floor, was the searchlight directing station with an apparatus that coordinated the movement of the searchlight beams with the movement of binoculars atop the mechanism. (Middle) In the powerhouse Gardiner Pat Croft diesel engines drove the Westinghouse generators for the searchlights; there was one combined unit for each searchlight and an additional standby engine in case of a breakdown. Beneath each gun were paired shell and charge magazines; in this underground magazine we can see the racks of shells and the dredger hoist at the far end which carried them up to the gun. (Bottom) This is No. 1 Gun Emplacement as seen from the O-Pip; it was built according to a standard design for Canadian and British coastal batteries. In the foreground is a protected gun crew shelter with stores room. The gun was placed on a central pivot mounting. At the foot of the steps is an emergency exit from the magazines and tunnel. In the background is the door for unloading the ammunition hoist.

Credit: Fort Rodd Hill National Historic Park and Department of National Defence.

Vancouver's Earliest Anti-Aircraft Defence: a Lewis machine-gun on a light mounting in 1940.
Credit: Jim Saddler.

The Ultimate Anti-Aircraft Defence: A battery of 3.7-inch guns at Ambleside in 1943.
Credit: Canadian War Museum, National Museum of Man, National Museums of Canada.

While gunners test fire a 2-pounder, naval anti-aircraft gun at Point Grey in August 1942, a comrade on the right plugs his ears. These guns were manufactured locally by the Dominion Bridge Company and were frequently demonstrated and tested at the fort.
Credit: Department of National Defence.

Public demonstration on Spanish Banks in April 1945 of Bofors light anti-aircraft guns of the 11th (Reserve) Anti-Aircraft Regiment, R.C.A. A battery under Capt. J.G.A. Hutcheson fired at a red nylon drogue towed by an airplane and shot off the target's tail.

Credit: 15th Field Artillery Regiment, R.C.A.

Back Together Again after 35 Years: Reunion of the Vancouver Coastal Gunners on May 11, 1975. (Top Left) Ken "Gunfire" Brown and Harry Mangles examine a Bofors shell in front of a picture of a gun on Yorke Island. (Top Right) The original commanders of the 85th Battery on Yorke Island in 1939: Majors J.E. Piercey and F.W. Guernsey. (Below) Veterans of the 58th Battery hold up a picture of themselves at Point Grey: (Front Row) - F.C. "Bud" Garrett, Nelson Darling, R. Theo DuMoulin, and Ted Cuddeford, (Back Row) - Len Cuddeford, Jerry Hatton, Doug Moore, Nelson Longeuay, Ken M. Bonnett, St. Clair McPherson, Ross Johnson, and A. "Gus" Clarke.

Credit: Peter N. Moogk.

"You kids! Get away from those Pacific Coast defences..."

A Comment in 1952 by Len Norris on the Decline of British Columbia's Coast Defences: back to muzzle-loaders in front of the Beatty Street Armouries.

Credit: Vancouver Sun.

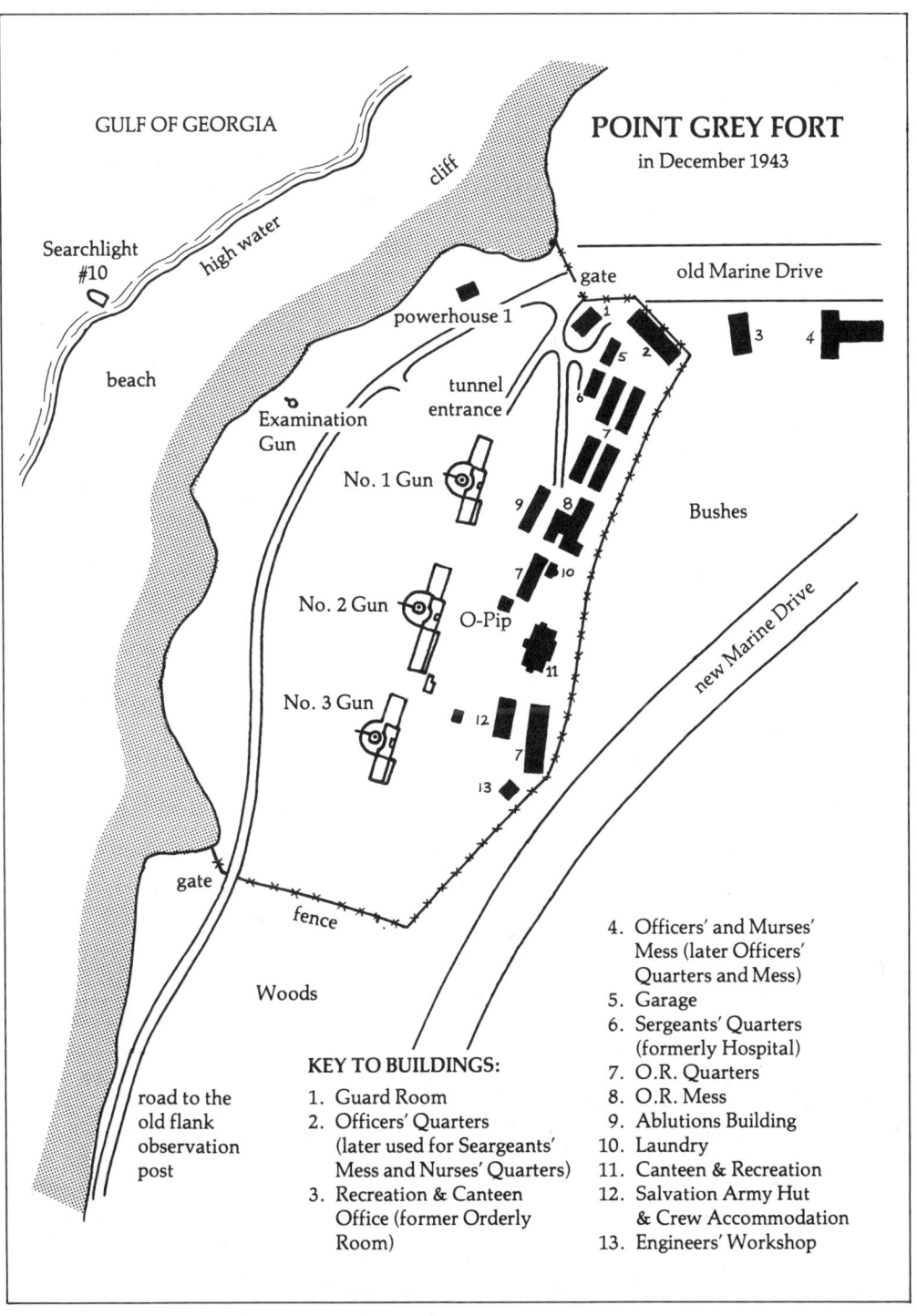

lems encountered with the 6-inch calibre guns on Point Grey were typical. Nos. 1 and 2 guns had been manufactured in 1899 and 1902 and the No. 3 gun, which was added in April 1941, dated from 1900. Its bore was so scored and pitted that the Fire Commander advised that "this gun is not to be fired with either one-half or full charge except in action (against an enemy vessel)."[5] The automatic sights on the guns could not be used for, as T. Murray Hunter explained, "it was understood that the guns had been brought from Fort McNab at Halifax...(and) the cams on the guns which, at short ranges controlled the correct relationship between elevation and range, had been cut for a battery height about 200 feet lower than that at Point Grey. The result was that the 'automatic' sights did not function for more than a year (until new ones were provided) and the guns had to depend on an alternative range-finder in a flanking observation post."[6] The guns, moreover, were on old Mark II mountings which allowed a maximum elevation of 15°; this limited their range to about eight miles. With 45° mountings the guns could have fired their 100-pound shells another two or three miles. The 4.7-inch guns in Stanley Park could accurately lob 45-pound projectiles over five miles. The 12-pounders of Narrows North had a shorter range but, at a possible 16 rounds a minute, their rate of fire was double that of the larger guns.

If the coastal guns left much to be desired, the anti-aircraft guns were simply desired. When the 1st Searchlight Regiment, R.C.A. was mobilized in late August 1939, it was divided into an anti-aircraft battery and a coast defence battery. The coast battery recruited men with a knowledge of electrical engineering and diesel engines to operate searchlights and the Gardner diesel generators that powered the lights. Others were given a course on diesel engines at Vancouver Technical School. These men found immediate employment while the anti-aircraft section, without guns to be assisted, passed the time studying the markings of foreign airplanes. This battery showed considerable initiative by constructing its own sensitive listening device to give advance warning of approaching aircraft. Radar (radio direction finding) had not yet come into general use. Major Harry Smith, O.C. of the battery, and other officers did the research for the sound detector and it was assembled by Bombardier Fred Adams, an expert electrician, and George Chester. The device consisted of a vertical bar and a horizontal bar with listening cones on a tripod base. The operator was linked to the cones with a stethoscope and the angle of the bars was adjusted to home in on the target's sound. The practice target used in the Bessborough Armouries was a brightly coloured toy airplane with an electrical buzzer attached to it. The airplane was carried about on a long pole to simulate different angles of attack.[7] Within a year the anti-aircraft battery was assigned to other duties.

When Canada declared war on Germany there were two obsolete 13-pounder anti-aircraft guns on the west coast. They were on Vancouver Island and they had no ammunition. From the point of view of safety, this was probably a good thing since one of the guns had a loose breech that fell open at inconvenient moments. When Major Treatt's proposals for the defence of the Pacific coast were being discussed in 1937-1938, the threat of shipborne aircraft was underestimated and surface vessels were considered the principal threat. The Sino-Japanese conflict and the Spanish Civil War showed how vulnerable cities were to aerial bombardment and Vancouverites feared that in war their city would be attacked with incendiary, gas and high explosive bombs. Vancouver was a major seaport, the terminus of two transcontinental railways, and a centre of light industry and population; it was an obvious target for an air raid. The danger had been long foreseen. In May 1938 the editors of the **Vancouver Daily Province** had castigated the Dominion government for providing the city with a coastal battery but no anti-aircraft defences.[8] In 1941-42 there were indeed Japanese submarines carrying aircraft off the west coast of North America. In January 1939 an unnamed officer of the 15th (Vancouver) Coast Brigade admitted that the coastal guns were only a deterrent to minor raids by naval vessels and that "what Vancouver needs - badly - are anti-aircraft guns (...) Without anti-aircraft guns, Vancouver would suffer severely both in casualties and in property damage."[9]

Canadian industry could not manufacture coastal guns, but light anti-aircraft weapons were within its capacity. Domestically-made 40-mm. Bofors guns appeared in 1942 and two were located at Point Grey in the autumn of that year. Until then the anti-aircraft defences of that battery consisted of Lewis and then Bren machine guns on special mountings and locally manufactured, naval 2-pounder "pom-poms" that were used for protection and weapons test in 1942-44. The numerous Bofors positions established around Vancouver harbour and the neighbouring airfields were replaced in mid-1943 by sixteen sites for 3.7-inch, heavy anti-aircraft guns. When these guns were fired the concussion caused windows to rattle throughout the city. The air defence batteries were manned by the 28th Anti-Aircraft Regiment, Royal Canadian Artillery.

So long bereft of an adequate air defence, the soldiers paid special attention to concealing the batteries from aerial observation. In their permanent positions the guns at Point Grey and in Stanley Park were shielded by parasol-like structures draped with net and coloured steel wool. Buildings were likewise camouflaged with paint and scrim. The concrete battery observation post at Ferguson Point in the park was artistically decorated with a large, painted evergreen tree.

Each of the Vancouver "forts" had hazards that were peculiar to its location. Sightseers were accustomed to having access to all parts of Stanley Park and they simply added the Ferguson Point battery and the adjoining camp to their list of curiosities to be visited. A board fence was therefore erected to screen the guns from the view of the rubberneckers and possible spies. One overzealous sentry there challenged the battery commander, Ken W. Hicks, with the astonishing statement "halt, who goes there, Major Hicks." Being next door to the campus of the University of British Columbia, the Point Grey battery was bound to pique the curiosity of the students, especially when they returned to their studies in the first year of the war. In October 1939 and despite the large sign reading "No Trespassing, by Order," a number ventured down old Marine Drive for a closer look. One of the culprits, Lionel Martin, told what happened:[10]

> *Soon the signs became more imposing and more numerous. Nevertheless, we were impelled by that little demon curiosity to take a look at the guns which command the Gulf from Point Grey.*
>
> *Suddenly, two soldiers came upon us and ordered us to halt. After giving us a verbal lashing on being illiterate, they decided to take us into custody. Since the barracks were on the other side of the fortifications, they found it necessary to make a detour through the woods in order that our knowledge of gunnery would not be augmented.*
>
> *As we were being marched back, we saw, coming through a trail, two other boys, who were soon to become our companions. Further on, three more groups of students were also victims of these circumstances, and now our little band had increased to ten, making it necessary for one of the soldiers to call for reinforcements.*
>
> *We were marched into the Barracks and held as prisoners in a hut with two sentries stationed at the door. I hoped that we would not be searched, for, if my chemistry notes were found on my person, they would certainly be thought cunningly conceived code messages. For a whole hour we were kept in suspense, wondering what was to happen (...) At last we were taken, individually, into the presence of three Commanding (sic)*

Officers, who were seated at a table. They not only asked us numerous questions but also emphasized the dangers of wandering around fortifications during war time.

After the interview we were marched separately to the gate and released. We departed, sadder but wiser, for we had acquired a respect for signs.[10]

Since October 13th, 1939 men of the 58th Battery had manned "Fort Steveston" as well as Point Grey. The fort was situated on the northwest corner of the fishing village, which was largely populated by Japanese-Canadians. The two 18-pounder field guns were located atop a waterlogged dike while the camp was 160 yards away. This distance and the proximity of so many Asians - a Chinese-Canadian family lived between the battery and the hutments - made the soldiers uneasy. It was thought that one of the Orientals might be a saboteur who would cut the telephone wires leading into the fort and, perhaps, do more than that. In the shadow of the Lions' Gate Bridge, the Narrows North camp seemed to be an ideal target for a "fifth columnist" with a bomb. Alas, it was not bombs but stones and bottles that rained upon the gunners below the bridge. Late night revellers bore some of the responsibility for this indignity though the gunners were inclined to blame the men employed in the north shore shipyards. It was galling to those who had volunteered for military service to see these civilians receive more pay and enjoy greater freedom than themselves. A wire mesh above the bridge railing reduced the hazard of falling debris and it was probably no accident that the gunners at the narrows were among the first troops in Canada to be issued with steel helmets.

On New Year's Day 1940 the gunners defending Vancouver and Yorke Island could look back on their work with satisfaction. The 1st Searchlight Regiment now numbered 204 all ranks and when active recruiting for the 15th Coast Brigade ended on October 25th, 1939, the regiment had 356 men on strength. These units were supported by the tiny and short-lived 1st Anti-Aircraft Regiment, R.C.A.; the 6th Field Company, Royal Canadian Engineers; and personnel of the Royal Canadian Corps of Signals and Service Corps. For a short period militia infantry regiments provided local defence for the gun batteries; the gunners then took over this responsibility for themselves. They had begun mobilization without stationery or communications and with insufficient equipment and uniforms. In 1942 when officers of the 15th recalled "the main lessons to be learnt from the mobilization in 1939" they emphasized the need for[11]

(a) *Suitable living accommodation to be provided in all Forts for personnel.*
(b) *Complete mobilization stores to be kept by he R.C.O.C. (Royal Canadian Ordnance Corps) in stock.*
(c) *Ammunition to be maintained in Forts, because all the Forts had no ammunition for several days after the order for the precautionary period.*
(d) *Fort Record Books must be kept up to date. There were no Fort Record Books at all for many of the Forts.*

Despite these shortcomings, everyone, including the untrained recruits, responded to the challenge of mobilization with enthusiasm and they did their best with whatever was available. In his New Year's message, Governor-General Lord Tweedsmuir paid this compliment to the militia: "The smoothness and efficiency with which they have taken up their wartime duties is a sample tribute to the qualities which have made Canadian soldiers famous throughout the world."[12]

CHAPTER 6

"Going Yorkey": Yorke Island, 1939-1945

One of a myriad of tiny islands on the coast of British Columbia with no past and little future, it had a decade in which it became the most vital island in a defence system and then waned with victory to anonymity. Yorke Island was to be scarred by roads, barracks, concrete gun and searchlight emplacements, generator facilities, magazines, as man prepared for war. This islet lying approximately 150 miles north-west of Vancouver, British Columbia, off the eastern tip of Hardwicke Island, occupies a commanding position at the junction of Johnstone Strait and Sunderland Channel. The nearest community of any consequence is the small logging town of Kelsey Bay, Vancouver Island, to the south-east across four miles of the often treacherous waters of Johnstone Strait. A scant 120 acres in area, this isolated wind-blown islet was to be home and sometimes Hell to as many as 260 men of the Royal Canadian Navy and the Canadian Army.

Captain George Vancouver was perhaps the first European to sight the Island when he named its larger neighbour to the west, Hardwicke Island, on July 13th, 1972. Captain G.H. Richards of H.M.S. **Hecate** in 1862 named the island Yorke which was the family name of the household of Hardwicke.[1] The **B.C. Pilot** of 1884 mentions it as "high, round, wooded and about a half mile in diameter".[2] The 1905 edition adds that it is "348 feet high to the tops of the trees".[3] Each description of the Island only serves to portray the poverty of this Island. In a Land Classification Report of 1925, it is pointed out that the area was rocky and broken, "exposed to heavy winds during the entire year"; also there was "very little water available during the summer months". The report concludes, "the area will make a home for a person who is engaged in fishing and logging in the vicinity and enough truck garden to supply his demands, but no living could be made from the area on account of poor market conditions". In 1925 a logger pre-empted the Island. When the property was inspected in August, 1926, he was "not in residence". There was a "shack, log and shakes, 8 feet by 10 feet valued at $50; shed, no sides, shake roof 14 feet by 20 feet, $30; and one-tenth acre partly cleared and seeded, $25; total value $95." The inspector commented, "The buildings are evidently the remains of an old logging camp. Residence at this time of year impossible, there being no water on the Island." By that time the logger had moved on. This was the last word of this meagre islet until 1937. The Treatt report of 1936 recommended Yorke Island as one of the sites which should be armed to cover the northern approach to Vancouver.

Yorke Island began its rise to prominence when on September 28th, 1937 the Island was placed under temporary reserve for the Department of National Defence. The October 1st issue of the **Vancouver Daily Province** gave this short report:[4]

B.C. Island Now Defense Reserve.

Victoria, Oct. 1. Yorke Island, a small rocky bluff in a commanding position at the northern entrance to Seymour Narrows in Johnstone Strait, has been reserved by the British Columbia Government for the department of national defence. An order-in-council to that effect was issued at the Legislative Buildings today.

The Island is just off the north end of Hardwick (sic) Island. Exact use to which the site will be placed by the federal department was not stated.

This, however, was not the first time that defences had been placed to guard this northern approach to Vancouver. At the outset of World War One, when von Spee's German Squadron posed a threat to the West Coast, a number of hasty measures were implemented to plug this northern passage. The following letter from Naval Headquarters Esquimalt dated October 12th, 1914, to Naval Headquarters in Ottawa outlines the precautions taken.[5]

I received your letter of Oct. 5th this morning, and am writing to explain the situation at Esquimalt as I understand it. During the last visit of the (HMS) Newcastle the question arose as to the possibility of the enemy's ships coming round the north end of Vancouver Island, and demanding ransom from Vancouver or Nanaimo.

This was considered feasible, and Captain Powlett undertook, on behalf of the Admiralty, to take certain precautions, the expense of which is to be borne by the Imperial Government. These precautions consist of:-

I   To lay mines (E.C.) (Electrically controlled) so as to block the passage between Vancouver Island and Malcolm Island near Pulteney Point.

II To improvise dropping gear for 14" torpedoes on motor launches; these boats will guard the entrance into the Johnstone Strait round the east end of Malcolm Island.

III To mount two 4" guns at Seymour Narrows in the hope of stopping any of the enemies' ships which might get into the Strait.

My instructions, received from Captain Powlett through Commander Hose, were to work with Commander Diggle of the Newcastle, *and to carry out the scheme as soon as possible. The question of the mines was first taken in hand.*

Sixteen old mine shells, lying on the submarine mining wharf at Esquimalt, were fitted and loaded with dynamite by members of the crew of the Newcastle; *the dynamite being ordered by Commander Diggle.*

On completion of this the mines were placed on board the C.G.S. (Canadian Government Ship) Newington, *with Lieutenant Burrard. A. Smith R.N. (retired) in charge, assisted by one torpedo instructor and one leading torpedosman from the* Newcastle *and the* Newington *proceeded to Alert Bay on Oct. 5th to await further orders. To guard the mine field a detachment of militia was sent from Vancouver on Oct. 7th, and two Maxim guns (ex* Algerine) *were sent from Esquimalt by motor launch "Davy Jones" to meet them at Alert Bay.*

> *The militia were instructed to place themselves under the orders of Lieutenant Smith who would transfer them to camp on Ellen Point or other suitable place, so as to command the proposed mine field.*
>
> *Motor launches for torpedoes were the next consideration. The Anglo-British Columbia Packing Company having offered to put their launches at the disposal of the Admiralty, three of their boats - Ivy Leaf, Laurel Leaf, & Holy Leaf were brought over to Esquimalt, and approved of by Commander Diggle if suitable dropping gear could be devised. This latter work was very efficiently carried out by the Chief Engineer of the yard and C.P.O Smallwood; successful runs were made by five torpedoes, which were available for this purpose.*

By early December 1914 the German naval threat had passed and all defences in this area had been withdrawn.

Treatt's recommendation in 1936 was promptly acted upon and soon plans were approved to arm Yorke Island. With amazing speed, work on the new battery began in late 1937. By July 1938 two Quick Firing (Q.F.) 4.7-inch guns had been mounted and test firing carried out. By no means new, these guns had been brought out from Halifax, Nova Scotia, where they had last been calibrated for wear of their barrels in April 1914! The tempo of construction and delivery of equipment, including the three searchlights necessary for night illumination of targets, limped almost to a halt as Nazi Germany now became a very real threat on the Atlantic. The guns and instruments destined for the West Coast were diverted to the Atlantic Coast forts. The provision of security and maintenance for the fort until an emergency arose was assigned to a small detachment of Permanent Force gunners from Esquimalt on a six month tour of duty.

The Second World War arrived early for the men of the 85th Battery of the 15th (Vancouver) Coast Brigade, Royal Canadian Artillery, who were to man the defences of Yorke Island. Although Canada did not officially declare war on Germany until September 10th, 1939, a number of units were called out earlier to guard vulnerable points and man the coast defences. The call to arms for the 85th Battery came at 4:00 a.m. on August 26th, 1939 and later at 8:00 a.m. the Battery was given 72 hours to prepare for the move to Yorke Island. The balance of the morning was spent notifying members of the 2:00 p.m. parade at Bessborough Armoury for those volunteering for service.[6] The next day was filled with issuing of uniforms and equipment, medicals, documentation and the clearing up of private affairs. On the evening of the 28th, Col. H.F.G. Letson, Commanding Officer, Military District No. 11 and Lt. Col. G.Y.L. Crossley, Commanding Officer of the 15th (Vancouver) Coast Brigade inspected the Battery commanded by Capt. F.W. Guernsey who then with his three officers and fifty-two men boarded two buses for Ballentyne Piere. On that wet rainy evening the H.M.C.S. **Comox**, a small, recently commissioned minesweeper, lay at the pier ready to transport the gunners to Yorke Island. After farewells to friends and relatives at the dock, the ship slipped its lines at 9:00 p.m. - making the men of the 85th Battery the first to go "overseas" in the Second World War. The cramped quarters of the minesweeper meant that most of the Battery slept out on deck. Ten o'clock the next morning saw the ship off the Island carefully sounding the tricky passage to the wharf. There to greet them were two gunners from the 5th Heavy Battery and one signalman. As the members of the militia, with their buttons impeccably shone, boots polished and leather bandoliers shining, caught sight of their reception party a look of horror and disbelief came over them - as they viewed the Permanent Force staff who stood before them wearing muddy gumboots, an odd mixture of sweaters and dryback coats with only the cap indicating that perhaps these men did belong to the military. It was not long before they too were to adopt this comfortable and practical form of dress.

The officers set about reconnoitering the Island and soon found the sleeping accommodation consisted of one barrack 18 feet by 50 feet, a kitchen, small hut 16 feet by 16 feet, radio signal hut, and the caretakers' five-room house occupied by the permanent staff detachment. The day was filled with a flurry of minor frustrations, lunch turned out to be a cold one as no stove pipe had been sent for the kitchen stove, and the tractor sent to haul supplies would not start. Men scurried about carrying materials from the wharf to the camp. At noon the coastal vessel **Border Prince** arrived with 4.7-inch ammunition which was unloaded by a battery work party. When it was time to bed down, not only was every available building used but two men had to sleep in the small fort launch, the York. Woodcutting parties were organized the next day to supply fuel for the various huts, a chore which would continue for several years. The tractor was finally started by a "cat" operator who was brought over from the Salmon River Logging Company, Kelsey Bay. The 4.7-inch ammunition was then moved up into the magazine in the fort area.

On September 3rd the Examination Service went into operation, responsible for controlling all marine movement and identifying all naval, merchant and small commercial and private vessels. This service was made up of one examination vessel which patrolled the strait north of the Island, and a naval signal detachment at the Battery Observation Post. The "X-Vic", as it was known, was usually not armed but was backed up by a designated gun of the fort if the need arose. An old 1918 minesweeper, H.M.C.S. **Armentieres**, served a few days as temporary examination vessel. Then came a group of small vessels of the Fishermen's Reserve to take over the role of examination vessel. The Fishermen's Reserve, unique to the West Coast, was formed within the Naval Service in 1938 to provide patrols on the West Coast should war in Europe force the transfer of the Pacific Squadron destroyers to the Atlantic. These vessels were for the most part privately owned fish boats and pleasure craft, some of which were equipped to carry out minesweeping duties. H.M.C.S. **Van Isle, Allaverdy** and **West Coast** were typical of those which served as examination vessels and also provided other services, such as transporting personnel and special supplies to and from Yorke Island. Support of the examination vessel regularly brought some feeling of urgency, as the guns were often called upon to bring to a stop an unheeding fishpacker or coastal vessel. In May of 1941 the Commander of the U.S. Army Engineer vessel Cavanaugh adopted a very insulting attitude as five rounds from the 6-pounder and one from the 4.7-inch were required to stop and properly identify his vessel.[7]

Number One gun was ready for action on September 4th, and with this began the lonely lookout watches maintained throughout hours of light and darkness, wind and rain, with eyes straining and voice ready to warn of the enemy's approach. Number Two gun was ready on September 9th, the day before Canada declared war. Although they were ready and could be fired, their effectiveness was seriously hampered as new auto-sight cams, which were custom-made for each particular gun site, were not ready. This problem arose from the guns originally having been mounted in Halifax at a different elevation above sea level. The 4.7-inch gun could fire a 45-pound projectile approximately five miles, enough to effectively close Johnstone Strait as it divided to the east and west of the Island. The first round fired in "anger" was a heave-to round which almost ended in a sinking. When the alarm rang, almost the entire garrison rushed up to the fort to witness the event. The layer-for line on the gun normally put on a deflection which would place the round well in front of the offending vessel; however, in this case the correction was in the wrong direction. The round landed a few feet from the stern, sending up a plume of water and a cheer from the battery. The skipper not wishing another that close heaved to at once.[8]

One of the most serious weaknesses in the choice of Yorke Island for a camp and fort was that there was no drinking water on the Island. This was to be a problem throughout the war. Every gallon of fresh water had to be brought to the Island and this was carried out in many varying and sometimes arduous fashions, even to the point of shipping it in ten gallon drums from Vancouver. During the early occupation of the Island water was often hand pumped from the wharf to the storage tank and one such delivery from H.M.C.S. **Armentieres** took ten hours. All this labour was climaxed by the discovery of a dead cat in the cistern, much to the consternation of the entire camp. Later on a water scow was used to pick up water from Hardwicke Island. Unexpected profit was wrung from the lack of water by one of the Royal Canadian Engineers stationed on the Island, whose duty was to check on the dam and water supply source which had been established on nearby Hardwicke Island. Soon it was noted he was very zealous in his maintenance of the water supply and often visited the Island; also he was observed shipping a number of boxes to Vancouver. On further investigation of the boxes, it was found that they were addressed to a well known Vancouver fur dealer. It would appear that much of his time spent maintaining the water system was in fact devoted to the care of his trapline. He had discovered that mink were abundant on Hardwicke Island![9]

On September 17th Captain Guernsey returned to Vancouver leaving the Battery in the hands of the Battery Captain until the arrival of Major J.E. Piercey on the 29th. Major Piercey, although a strict disciplinarian, was a popular officer who had joined the Regiment at its formation. He was to command the Island for the first difficult year of new construction, battling shortages of food, equipment, proper quarters, and the ever present spectre of boredom. He later was to have a second tour as battery commander, the only commanding officer to do so. He insisted on a morning parade in full dress on the wharf, the only flat area suitable; but also gave the men leave to hunt or fish in the area. This struck a happy balance of work and play, maintaining good morale despite hardships. As ammunition supplies dwindled through practice and the firing of stopping rounds Major Piercey requested replenishment. After several hasteners and no results he sent a message direct to Ottawa: "We have two and a half minutes ammunition remaining at normal rates of firing -- what do we do then, throw rocks?" His knuckles were rapped for circumventing the normal chain of command, but his message brought the desired results and the ammunition was soon on its way.[10]

The camp, with barracks, kitchen, canteen, drill hall, administration, hospital, quartermaster stores etc., was situated near the wharf on the south side of the Island. The fort itself was perched atop a rocky bluff which rose sharply to approximately 180 feet above the western shore. It consisted of two 4.7-inch guns, the Battery Observation Post, magazine, war shelter, gun stores, and powerhouse. The three searchlight emplacements were sited along the western shore. With a range of 9300 yards the guns guarded the western passage, that was 3500 yards wide, between Yorke and Vancouver Island and a 2600 yard channel between Yorke and the mainland of British Columbia. The fort's three searchlights did not arrive until early 1941, leaving the guns virtually blind should they have had to fight a night engagement. Once installed, the lights had an approximate effective range of 3500 yards, which of course was dependent on weather conditions.

There was a constant flow of men to and from the Island as replacements arrived for those posted to other duties, courses and overseas. While the artillery composed the greatest number on the Island, there were also personnel from the Medical Corps who staffed the small hospital, Royal Canadian Engineers, Royal Canadian Signal Corps, Royal Canadian Army Service Corps and, of course, the Royal Canadian Navy. For the first two years, until they were absorbed into the 15th Coast Regiment, the searchlights were operated by the 3rd Searchlight Battery (Coast Defence) of the 1st Searchlight Regiment, R.C.A. The infantry also played an important role in the defence of the Island and had responsibility for repelling enemy landings on the Island, allowing the gunners freedom to man and fire their guns. The 2nd Battalion, The Canadian Scottish Regiment from Victoria, supplied the first infantry platoon which served until late 1940. Men of the Veterans Guard of Canada, composed of First World War veterans who were mainly over age or medically unfit for overseas and regular service, also served as local defence infantry. These old sweats performed many unrewarding but necessary duties to allow the younger, fit men to go overseas. Later Home Defence conscript units such as the Canadian Fusiliers were to provide infantry protection on the Island. Every aspect of defence seemed to be thwarted by the Island's isolated position. Even the sand to fill sandbags for the listening posts on the beach and machine gun emplacements on top of searchlight towers had to be brought on to the Island. One tragic accident occurred as a work party set out to pick up a load of sand from a nearby bay on Hardwicke Island. One of the lifeboats from the C.P.R. ship **Prince Robert** was often used in transporting everything from water to sand, and the party had loaded it to capacity. The sea was fairly calm but the lifeboat, heavily laden and low in the water, took on water as some small swells lapped over the gun whales. Those on the lifeboat tried to pull the boat up to the Service Corps towing vessel and to jump on before the boat sank. The lifeboat plummeted to the bottom just as they were about to board the towing vessel, taking with it one man whose leg had become entangled in a rope. His body was never recovered. The others who had jumped into the water were rescued.[11]

The first two years were characterized with an ever-growing feeling that if you wanted any action Yorke Island was hardly the place to find it. Almost every excuse to leave the Island was tried. Men would volunteer for anything that would take them off the Island. One such attempt is related by F.C. "Bud" Garrett who upon hearing that volunteers were needed for Z Force, immediately applied even though he had no idea what it was or where it would take him. It was a stormy evening as he left the Island in the small fort launch to rendezvous with the southbound Canadian National Steamship. Approaching the larger ship, the launch was suddenly picked up by the winds and sea and battered against the hull of the CN ship. Lt. Garrett scrambled up the ship's ladder just in time, as a few more minutes of battering would have smashed the launch to pieces. Upon arriving in Vancouver he was outfitted with tropical clothing, given a medical examination and numerous shots, and more documentation. Then a message arrived that no replacement was available and he was to return immediately to Yorke Island. Looking back today, the recall saved him from a little too much action - as Z Force turned out to be the ill-fated Canadian force which was captured by the Japanese at Hong Kong on Christmas Day 1941.[12]

The emotions and mental balance of some men were disturbed by the isolation, the boredom of routine duties, lack of recreation, and the inhospitable nature of the weather. George, the canine mascot who loved to be up and around when the guns were fired was shot by a gunner who was promptly arrested and given 28 days in detention. Another gunner committed suicide on the boat while returning to the Island, while two others were apprehended as stowaways aboard the coastal ship **Border Prince** as they tried to shake the mud of the Island from their feet. A tale of one man wishing to be sent back to Vancouver is recounted as follows: as the medical officer was making a routine inspection of the kitchen he noticed in a dark corner two large washtubs, one upside down on the other and as he glanced at them, the top one slowly opened and closed with two eyes peering from the opening. When asked what was going on, the cook replied, "Oh he's just going 'Yorkey', he thinks he's a clam." A song written by Gunner R.M. "Red" Ramsay expressed the sentiments of many serving on the Island.

GOING YORKY (Sic)

When you're feeling kinda blue and you're melancholy too
  And you think the whole world's wrong
And you go around in a daze, and your mind is in a haze,
  And the days are sad and long;
You want to argue with the Sergeants
  And growl at Bombardiers and you think you're in a jail,
You get dopey in the head, and your spirits fall like lead,
  Then you know you're going Yorky!

You feel just like a slave, when you forget to shave,
  And you get put on the peg;
You think by guzzling beer, you'll make trouble disappear
  And then you try to drive a keg;
And you always start to grieve, when someone goes on leave
  Just because you can't go too,
You get softening of the brain, for you cannot stand the strain,
  Then you know you're going Yorky!

The gas lamps you will find, will surely make you blind,
  And you'll find we're all screw-balls;
If you're on this Island long, tho' you think your mind is strong
  You'll soon be climbing trees and walls;
Now, all of this is true, for we are wacky too,
  As you may well perceive,
In taking up your time, and in handing you this rhyme,
  You can see that we've gone Yorky![3]

To give the men a break from this isolated posting there was a rotation with the Vancouver batteries of the Regiment. The first major rotation took place in October 1940 when Major R.T. DuMoulin brought the 58th Battery from Point Grey and took command from Major Piercey, who had commanded since late September 1939.

By December 1941 the only changes in the defences were the installation of the three Canadian General Electric 60-inch searchlights and the mounting of one 6-pounder, used as the stopping gun for the examination service. This gun served to conserve the heavier ammunition and to avoid wear on the barrels of the larger guns. There were still no adequate anti-aircraft defences here, or elsewhere in B.C. Several old World War One Lewis machine-guns provided token defence against low flying aircraft.

The searchlight operators were not too long in discovering a method of augmenting the army ration. As fall approached and the annual migration of ducks took place, the operators would erect a net on top of the emplacement and wait until dusk. As the ducks flew down the channel, on flashed a search-light and down its beam flew the ducks, only to veer upwards to avoid the light and fly into the net. They were then popped into a sack and whisked away to the men's kitchen.[14]

The attack on Pearl Harbor on December 7th, 1941, suddenly brought the role of West Coast defences back into sharp focus and every effort was made to meet the projected scales of attack as outlined in the Treatt Report. The prospect of some form of attack now entered the thoughts of many. In anxious minds logs and floating debris were transformed into periscopes and submarines; strange noises turned into a possible enemy landing party and the whole garrison frequently took up their battle stations. Yorke Island now took on a much more important role and it was decided that her armament should be increased. With no surplus guns in Canada and those on order in England unlikely to arrive for at least another year a straight trade was made with the two 6-inch guns at Ferguson Point in Stanley Park, Vancouver and the two 4.7-inch ones at Yorke Island. To keep both batteries operational only one gun from each was to be moved at a time. The changeover was to take place at the end of June 1942 and early July. Tension was mounting at this time as the Japanese were now in the position of being able to launch a hit and run raid. Dutch Harbour, Alaska was bombed on June 3rd, 1942, and on the evening of June 20th the Japanese submarine I26 fired approximately seventeen projectiles at the Estevan Point Lighthouse on the West Coast of Vancouver Island. This was to be the only direct attack on Canada in over one hundred years. A code message of 1072 letters received at battery headquarters on June 24th required one and a half hours to decode. Much to the dismay of the cipher clerk it contained the details of the attack on Estevan Lighthouse which had been broadcast for all to hear over every private radio on the island the day before![15] In the midst of the confusion of dismantling the first 4.7-inch gun 25 anti-aircraft gunners arrived from the 6th Light Anti-Aircraft Regiment's 30th Battery commanded by Major Connie Smyth of hockey fame. They were to provide the first real air defence with two Bofors 40 mm guns. The next day (June 26th) at 4:00 p.m. the first 6-inch gun arrived by scow and after waiting for the rising tide it was unloaded by midnight. After much hard work by all available men the 6-inch was mounted and ready for action at 9:00 p.m. on June 28th. The second 6-inch arrived July 1st and both guns were in action and test fired on July 3rd.[16] The fort now had a gun capable of firing approximately seven 100 pound rounds per minute, a distance of eight miles. The fort had now reached its peak in armament and no major additions or removal of equipment were to occur although some surveys for siting coast artillery radar were carried out in 1944. A continuous improvement of quarters, messes and even some new buildings was carried on well into 1945 and by the cessation of hostilities there were sixty-two buildings of various types on the Island.

A constant effort was made to provide entertainment and recreation and the YMCA supervisors with their bingo, films, and assistance in publishing of the Island paper known as **The New Yorker**, sometimes known as the mouthpiece of the "Rock", played a large part in keeping the morale up. Morale was even more difficult to maintain as more than sixty percent of the battery were Home Defence conscripts. On an inhospitable island, in the army against their wish, many of these men were far from homes in the Prairies and Eastern Canada. The work of Padre Alan D. Greene who acted as chaplain to the fort throughout the war was rather unique as he also continued to serve with the Columbia Coast Mission of the Church of England. The Mission's boats the **Columbian**, **John Antle** and **Rendezvous** were frequent visitors to the island. Padre Greene describes a typical visit to the Island in the spring of 1944.[17]

I spent three days at York Island among the troops, and on Sunday had a very hearty church parade. It's the one place I am sure of a congregation of any proportions. Something like the chaplain in certain state institutions. But in spite of the parade being compulsory, I really believe a high percentage of the soldiers enjoy it, and for the few who come to the voluntary Communion services, there is unquestionably real profit. I enjoy the session in the men's hutments. There are lads from all over Canada there, and sometimes, not often, the visit goes deeper than happy talk and fellowship as soldiers. It is good to sit for an hour in the darkness of the O.PIP (Battern Observation Post), and chat with three or four men who are on watch, and perhaps get pretty close to their hearts as the visit goes on. I have been padre here since September, 1939, and have seen great changes in the place and in the personnel, and in these four and a half years made many friends...

Twenty-four hour manning of the guns and lights continued along with regular firing practices, the last of which took place August 10th, 1945. By this time an air of expectancy hung over the Island as the war drew to a close and their release from "confinement" on the Island was at hand. During the daily inspection of quarters by the Battery Captain on August 14th, he found all available radios turned on in hope of catching the news of the impending surrender. At 4:00 p.m. the BBC radio announced Japan's acceptance of surrender and the General Alarm siren was blown and an order was issued that Sunday routine would follow the next day.[18] The moment they had been waiting for had arrived at last. However, it would be another 12 days before the Examination Service would cease its operational role and one more day before orders would relieve the gunners from their watches. Yorke Island had come to the finale of its operational role almost six years from its beginnings as the northern anchor to the Vancouver defences.

Almost immediately procedures for disbanding the battery and the return of equipment and stores to Vancouver were prepared. Guns were cleaned for the last time and put in maintenance. On October 17th, 1945, at 11:00 a.m. the last of the battery personnel with Major A.G. Macdougall left the Island aboard the Army Service Corps boat **General MacKenzie,** ending the longest occupation of a fort by a battery of the 15th Coast Regiment. Thankless but vital, the task was well done.

CHAPTER 7

Hurry up and Wait

In retrospect, it might appear that since Vancouver's defences were meant to repel naval attacks and since Japanese submarines apparently did not enter the Strait of Georgia the protective measures were a wasted effort. By themselves the coastal batteries were a deterrent to raiders. "Who's to say what would have happened if the city had been undefended?" asked R. Theo DuMoulin, an officer of the 15th. It is important to recall that the forts performed a variety of services in addition to guarding the port. To an anxious populace, they were evidence that some protection against a surprise attack was being provided. It has also been suggested that the United States might have intruded to ensure its own security if Canada had not acted to defend her territory.[1] The psychological and strategic value of the coastal batteries can be debated, but what is beyond question are the practical services the home defences performed in training men for service overseas and in enforcing port security regulations during the Second World War.

Early in 1940 the Vancouver newspapers ran a series of morale-boosting articles on the airmen and soldiers guarding British Columbia. One month before the fall of France a correspondent was unfortunate enough to describe the Victoria-Esquimalt gun batteries as "miniature Maginot Lines."[2]   On February the 14th Peter Stursberg of the Vancouver **Daily Province** was allowed to observe a firing practice from the flank observation post at Point Grey. Though the **Province** spoke of "heavy guns...somewhere in Vancouver" being "groomed for business," the facts were more prosaic. Major C.K. Rosebrugh, second-in-command of the 15th Coast Brigade, reported to area headquarters **"14th February, A.M.** One-inch aiming rifle practice at Point Grey. Visibility was quite poor, especially the left half of the zone where the maximum was about 4,000 yards. A total of 75 rounds of one-inch aiming was (sic) fired in five series at ranges between 2,100 and 2,300 yards."[3]   The target consisted of two floats representing a destroyer towed by a launch in the Gulf of Georgia off Point Grey and this practice was, for most of the men, the first time that they had fired the guns to seaward. In addition to the aiming rifles, there were sub-calibre tubes for a 3-pound shell that could also be inserted into the main bore. The tubes permitted live-firing drill at little cost and without wear to the gun's barrel. A

3-pounder shoot occurred on the following day when no reporters were present. For all practice firings maritime traffic was forewarned by the press to stay clear of the target zone and, as an additional warning, a red flag was flown from the battery flagstaff that customarily carried the Union Jack.

It was hard to get excited about the firing of a one-inch aiming rifle and Peter Stursberg did his best to dramatize the event.[4]

> As the order rang out, the men in the O-Pip (observation post) became tense. Before that we had been chatting and glancing idly out at the two dots moving slowly across the grey sea.
>
> A bombardier, his eye glued to the range finder, had kept on repeating "on sight," and a gunner had kept on calling out the calibrated readings "2200...2250...2300...-2325," until their voices had taken on the monotonous quality of the fishing boat that puttered somewhere beneath us. The radio in the room behind hummed.
>
> I was waiting impatiently for the fortress guns to open fire at those barges being towed by a tug out at sea, when someone who had been peering through field glasses said the red flag was up on the ship.
>
> "Target destroyer moving north represented by floats," the major (R.T. DuMoulin) called out. "Target destroyer moving north represented by floats," the telephone operator repeated.
>
> Suspense gripped the O-Pip which seemed like the bridge of a ship standing high on the bluff overlooking the sea. The range finders kept on calling out the varying distances of the target.
>
> A soldier moved the hands of a large dial. "That's the telegraph," the colonel (Gordon Y.L. Crossley) whispered in my ear. "It sends back the range to the guns."
>
> "Open 100 right 2," the major called out. "Open 100" meant that the shells were to fall parallel but 100 yards apart, and "right 2" was its location, the colonel explained.
>
> The telephone operator leaned forward and called out "Shot 1." We listened intently and heard a soft "plop," and a few seconds later saw a tiny splash beyond the target.
>
> "Plus 1," the major said, plus meaning that the shell had landed beyond the target. "The two dots (of the target) are a destroyer's length apart," said the colonel, "so that if a shell falls in between we have a direct hit."
>
> "Plus 2," the major said, as there was another tiny splash. "Close 100," he ordered, which meant the guns were to fire 100 yards apart but in line. "Plus and minus," he said, as two shells fell on each side of the black dots.
>
> In the colonel's car we drove the quarter of a mile or so from the observation post to the emplacement and arrived just as steel-helmeted crews rushed to man the guns for the second burst of firing.
>
> The order to fire rang out from the high command post, overlooking the guns, and the long grey muzzles swung slowly into range. Straddled on each side of the gun two men peered through the telescopic sights. The sergeant brought his arm down.
>
> There was a short staccato crack and a long hissing whistle. The guns had sub-calibre tubes and were firing one-inch one pound shells instead of the heavy snub-nosed shells that were stored ready for use under the gun platforms. That's why there was no ear-splitting roar, and that's why few people knew there was any firing going on around Vancouver yesterday. It wasn't spectacular, but it saved the taxpayers a lot of money.
>
> The muzzles of the guns moved electrically up and down after each salvo. "That's for loading," the sergeant said. "With these B.B. bullets we don't need it; but we're doing it for practice."

The guns are fired by a pistol trigger beside the sights. When a full charge is used recruits usually attach a 30-foot lanyard to the trigger, but experienced artillerymen fire the monster as if they were shooting a .22 (calibre rifle).

In late June 1942, on the eve of Army Week, reporters were again admitted to the coastal forts around Vancouver. "Gunners Want to See Action" ran the heading of one report with considerable understatement. "At strategic points along the waterfront of the Lower Mainland," it went on, "...the camouflaged muzzles of the heavy guns point seaward, ever guarding the straits, gulf, and bay that are the channels for our seaborne shipping. In barracks nearby live the soldiers who man the guns, who spend endless hours rehearsing for the few minutes of intense excitement they hope will come their way some day. And if the Japanese, undaunted by the disastrous results that accompanied their attempted submarine sneak raid on the harbour of Sydney, Australia, several weeks ago, try repeating it here, the boys will have their opportunity. Lieut. Col. G.Y.L. Crossley, officer commanding the 15th (Vancouver) Coast Brigade, and these secluded forts, is well satisfied that his boys would provide a warm welcome for such uninvited guests."[5] Two days later, on June 29th, Lieut. Col. Alfred O. Hood of the 5th (B.C.) Coast Regiment arrived in Vancouver to take over command of the 15th. Further changes were to come. In mid-July the brigade assumed the new name of 15th (Vancouver) Coast Regiment, R.C.A., and absorbed the 3rd Searchlight Battery (Coast Defence) - all that remained of the 1st Searchlight Regiment in the Vancouver area - giving the unit a total strength of 776 all ranks. The regiment was now responsible for the maintenance and operation of the forts' searchlights and diesel generators. 720 men were in the Vancouver defences in October 1942. Of those 60 were in the regimental headquarters and the rest were distributed as follows: 31st Coast Battery - Stanley Park (150), Narrows North (90), Point Atkinson (80); 58th Coast Battery - Point Grey (250) and Steveston (90).

In a war that seemed to have passed them by, the coastal gunners craved some escape from the tedium of garrison duties. Most of the welcome diversions were provided by the port examination service. Early in September 1939 the port of Vancouver had come under the authority of the Royal Canadian Navy and "Public Traffic Regulations" were issued to control vessels entering or leaving the harbour. On Point Atkinson the navy maintained the Port War Signal Station that received advance warning by radio of major warships and a lookout that identified all inbound naval vessels. From Point Atkinson lighthouse to the tip of Point Grey ran the imaginary "Examination Line" which marked off the harbour area where no unauthorized movement of ships was permitted. A half mile or more to the west of this line were two naval launches known as X-Vics or examination vessels. A third X-Vic lay a mile off Ferguson Point. These vessels flew a distinctive flag of white and red horizontal bars with a blue border. Incoming merchant ships were required to cut speed when approaching the examination line and to identify themselves to the X-Vics with signal pennants. No private radio transmissions were allowed within the controlled area. Shipowners and shipping agents were expected to inform the naval authorities in advance of expected arrivals and give them the particulars of each vessel. Suspect and unheralded ships were escorted to the examination anchorage situated under the guns of Stanley Park for a detailed inspection. When a vessel was cleared for admission into the inner harbour it was informed of the signal of the day and the gun batteries were notified to let it pass. Simpler rules applied to small craft of less than 120 tons displacement. Tugs, fishing boats and pleasure craft that regularly used the port had a recognition number painted on their sides and they were to identify themselves to the Point Atkinson signal station in passing. They then proceeded to the patrol boat (XV3) in English Bay to obtain clearance to pass

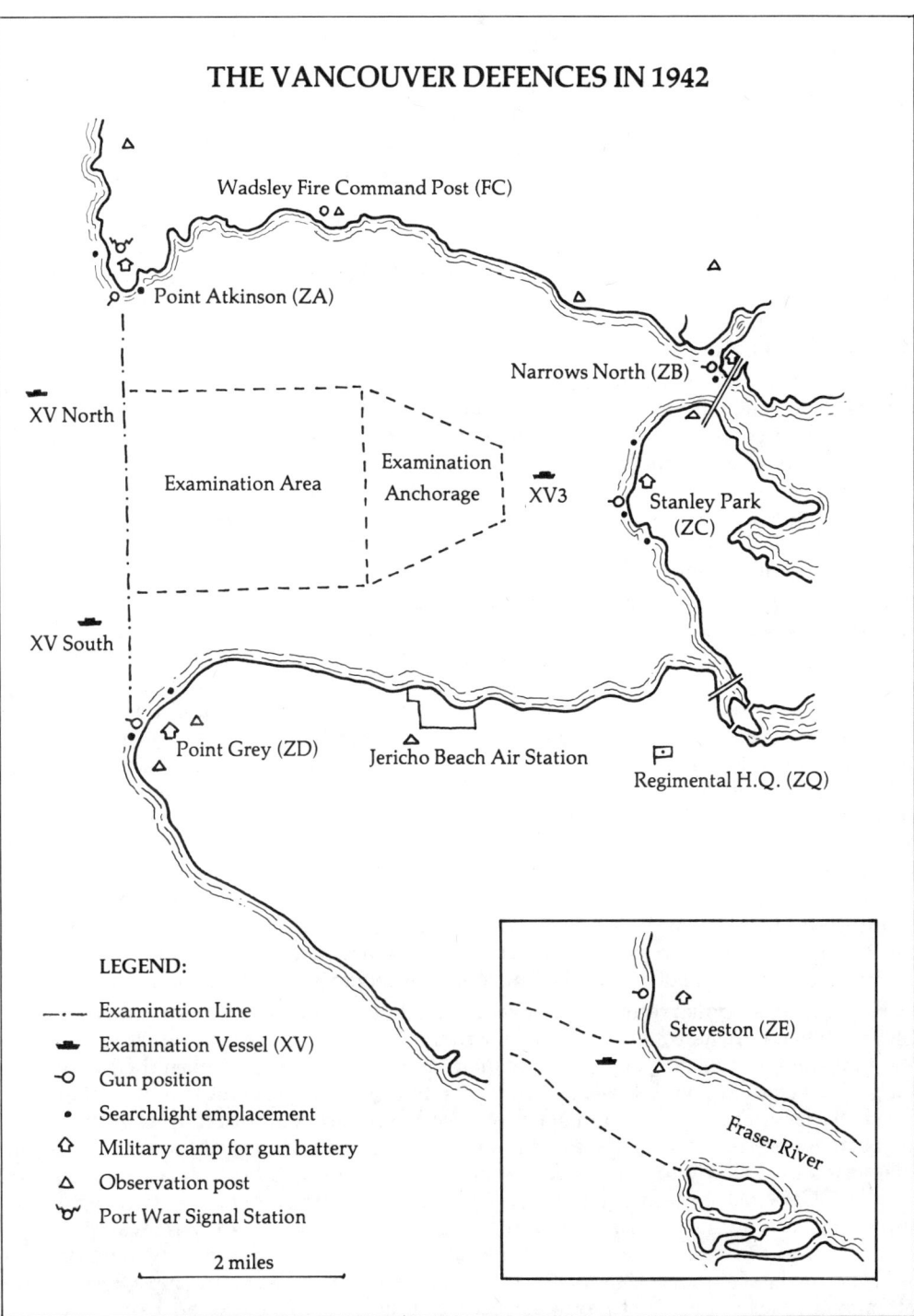

the First Narrows. "Failure to comply strictly with these Regulations," warned the navy, "will be considered a hostile act and will be dealt with accordingly."[6] Disobedience of the rules or the orders given by the examination vessels rendered a vessel liable to be fired upon. A series of 2's by aldis lamp, sound or radio was the signal to the Point Grey or Point Atkinson gun battery to fire a stopping round ahead of the delinquent vessel. Persistent noncompliance brought the order "fire for effect" which, in layman's language, meant "sink the b_____!" A few fishermen and Sunday sailors learned this lesson the hard way.

Point Grey had been the original "examination battery." In September 1939 a Q.F. 6-pounder Hotchkiss was mounted between the other guns, on the former roadway, for use as a heave-to gun. The gunners in all the forts looked forward to opportunities to fire a plugged round into the water ahead of some miscreant. At Point Grey it was an unofficial rule that whoever reached the 6-pounder first after the order to take post would have the privilege of firing the weapon. When it became evident that a Boer War veteran named Triggs took special delight in discharging the gun, the younger men lagged behind to allow him to gallop ahead of them. For negligent shipowners there was another rule: they had to pay the cost of the stopping rounds fired at their vessels. In 1942 Captain James W. Jamieson was returning to Vancouver from Rivers Inlet. His fishing boat was the **Georgie**; it had been seized by the government from a Japanese-Canadian and sold to Jamieson for $300. Captain Jamieson had no radio set and he ignored the identification rules when entering Burrard Inlet. For this he was not only fired upon but he later received a bill for $42.50 - the price of one heave-to round.[7]

It was not easy for the men on Point Grey to keep an eye on the examination line and the patrol vessels. The shallows created by Spanish Banks on the north side of the point forced ships to take the deep channel along the opposite shore. As a consequence, most of the maritime traffic was 6,000 to 7,000 yards away from the examination battery. On top of this, in every season except summer, fog and mists developed around Point Grey and obscured the view of the harbour entrance. Again, remember that radar was not available to overcome this difficulty. To solve the problem a second examination gun was established below Point Atkinson lighthouse in August 1942. This was a Mark I 18-pounder like those at Steveston though this gun was on a pivot supported by a concrete base. The gunners stationed there since October 1941 had, until then, been exclusively concerned with the two searchlights on the point. As the tide of war turned against Japan it was decided to reduce the examination service to one patrol boat (XV-North) and the Point Atkinson gun. This was done on December 29th, 1943. On March 2, 1944 Vancouver's examination service was ended. The two guns that had given force to the port's security regulations were dismantled in the following summer.

The firing of stopping rounds was never limited to Point Grey and Point Atkinson. Fort Steveston was designated an examination battery though it was nearly useless in this role; the guns were a thousand yards from the main shipping channel and when the patrol boat intercepted craft both vessels were often hidden from view by buildings on the waterfront. The batteries at Stanley Park and Narrows North were also authorized to challenge ships that had not been cleared by the examination service. Identification at the entrance to the inlet was hampered by fog and heavy weather which forced XV-North to take refuge in Caulfeild Cove. At the beginning of the war the battery commanders were reluctant to use their guns to enforce the rules and the operators of small craft were casual about observing security regulations. At Narrows North the new order seems to have begun on a Friday night, February 15th 1940 to be exact, when the merchant ship **Queen Maud** attempted to make port "with an incorrect signal hoisted." A 12-pounder on the gantry fired a plugged shell ahead of her bow and though the ship stopped engines at once she was carried under the bridge by the current. Many north shore residents telephoned the newspapers to find out if the shot they had heard had been fired at an enemy craft.[8] Narrows North was notorious for its accidents. The guns were always kept loaded and a block of wood was used to separate the shell's primer from the electrical firing circuit. When a bombardier was explaining the features of the guns to a recruit he removed the block and then, without thinking, slammed the breech shut. The circuits were live and the weapon fired, sending a round whizzing past the Point Atkinson lighthouse. The incident that still causes embarassed laughter among veterans of the 15th Coast occurred on September 13th, 1942. This was when the gunners proved that they could sink a ship, albeit a friendly one.

D. Ken Brown had taken over command of the Narrows North detachment in late June 1942 and he believed in a firm application of the port security regulations. With the approval of Col. Hood, the guns came into action. The firing of heave-to rounds provided useful training for the troops and it cowed the fishermen into conforming with the wartime rules. "Once heaving tasted the idea of using the rules to provide practice," recalls Ken Brown, "then, on the slightest opportunity, when it was permissible for us to fire, even though we suspected rather strongly that they were friendly, (...) we fired that round, as the rules called for it, two degrees ahead of the target so that the splash could be seen. It was more realistic than the normal gun drill." This gave young Lieut. Brown a reputation: "the nickname I acquired, 'Gunfire Brown,' was because during the first month that I was in command I remember firing something like thirty-one rounds."

Ken Brown remembered that on that fateful Sunday afternoon, when "the famous or infamous misadventure" happened, it was overcast and windy. A fish-packer chugged in past Point Atkinson and ignored all the signals to identify himself. As the boat approached the narrows, the fort there received an order to fire a stopping round. "The message came from the examination vessel stationed just off Point Atkinson," states Ken, "I think it was a radio message. The battery was at rest normally until an alarm was sounded and that was activated by messages received from the examination vessel. We were away from the gantry and had to run several yards gathering our helmets and equipment. We arrived on the scene rather disturbed." When the gun was fired "we had the desired result: the fish boat stopped."[9] The plugged shell, however, had not stopped. Instead of kicking up a splash and sinking, the round hit a wave and ricocheted across the water at an oblique angle. In its path lay a freighter recently launched by Burrard Dry Docks and now undergoing speed trials over a measured mile in English Bay. This was the 9,600 ton **Fort Rae**. E.L. "Paddy" Copeland, who was on the beach at Ambleside with his wife, saw what was happening despite the haze on the water. "When we saw this shot go skipping across the water, I said to my wife 'it's going to hit that freighter' (...) they hit it amidships right at the waterline (...) it went right through it. That's the one and only time I saw that happen."[10] The damage was greater than anyone imagined. The non-explosive shell had entered the No. 3 hold, just forward of the engine room, and left a neat hole above the waterline on the near side of the **Fort Rae**. Yet unseen by those present, the shell tumbled after impact and, striking sideways, it punched out a larger hole on the far side of the hull **below** the waterline.[11] Ken Brown picks up the story: "there was no alarm until they finished that testing run and turned to come into the (inner) harbour, at which time the hold was flooding and there was obviously panic. They beached the hull just inside the Lions' Gate Bridge (...) I wasn't very popular with the ship's captain and Col. Hood wasn't very pleased with the incident."

The beached ship was subsequently patched up and floated off the north shore tidal flats to be returned to the builder's yard. An army court of inquiry was set up to investigate the episode and the charges of Captain Semple and his crew that the gunners had deliberately fired three shells at their ship, including a shot through the rigging. "Fortunately for me," remarks Ken Brown, "we were able to prove that we had only fired one round legally and within the rules." A.F. Menzies, retired chief engineer of the Burrard Dry-Docks, remembers a distressed gunner from the fort saying "For God's sake, don't talk about it; there's been enough misery." The archivist of the shipyard, J.R. Holden, describes the accident as "quite a joke - it was supposed to be a military secret."

As the years passed and the social composition of the coast artillery units in Canada changed, morale tended to fall. At the beginning of the Second World War men were eager to join the army and they were happy to perform their new duties. The war, after all, had ended the economic depression that had blighted the lives of a generation. Young men who had survived on charity and public relief work were offered good food, a bed, clean clothes and a measure of self-respect by the armed forces. "Thank-you, thank-you" said Arne P. Knudsen, a Danish immigrant who had been on the breadlines, as food was heaped on his plate in the mess. "Don't thank me," replied the dispenser of food, "thank Hitler." In June 1941 the press interviewed men stationed in Vancouver's coastal batteries. "Finest In Comfort and Food Is Provided for Soldiers In Dominion's New Army" was the heading for Don Mason's report in the **Vancouver Daily Province**. He spoke to a recruit who had joined up two weeks before and who "was agreeably surprised to find such excellent living conditions in a Canadian army camp. 'I had been prepared for something quite different' (said the recruit). 'You see, I had heard about 'lousy' army grub...you know the sort of thing. But I have found that the grub in this man's army is as good as, or better than, that served in the average Canadian home.'" For the benefit of his readers, the reporter copied down the menu for that day:

BREAKFAST - *Rolled wheat, bacon and boiled eggs, toast and honey, coffee.*

LUNCH - *Vegetable soup, roast beef, roasted potatoes, boiled carrots, bread pudding and custard sauce, bread, tea.*

SUPPER - *Hamburgers, fresh tomatoes, boiled potatoes, baked apple, tea.*

"It's fresh milk for breakfast," added the reporter, "canned milk for other meals. A box of British Columbia's famous apples is kept in the kitchen at all times. A soldier can have as many as he wants as often as he wants."

The enthusiastic recruit encountered by Mason at the Stanley Park camp, where the Third Beach parking lot is presently located, also praised army beds: "Our bunks are swell, and boy! You don't know what cleanliness means until you join the army." The reporter agreed that "the hutments are cozy and comfortable; the beds are cots in tiers of two - with springs. A soldier in the last war wasn't so lucky. He slept on a bed spring of wooden slats over two-by-fours." For the recreation of the troops, Mason observed "a well-used horseshoe pitch" and "a Salvation Army hut (that) provides a canteen, table games, a reading, writing and sitting room."[12]   The **Vancouver Sun** reporter found "the men off duty...putting away 'pop' and chocolate bars in the Salvation Army hut where coffee and doughnuts fill any empty stomach space between meals and after hours. The hut also provides free motion pictures, shows and games." The gunner he interviewed rated comradeship or "darned good company" high among the benefits of army life.[13]

In their zeal to assist recruiting, the newspapers painted a rosy picture of military life. For some the immediate benefits of enlistment were outweighed by discomforts experienced by the "concrete gunners" in British Columbia. A few drifters who had signed up at the beginning of the war tried to obtain a discharge after one winter by refusing innoculations; after that the medical officer jabbed and then asked for consent. Desertions increased as the years passed. There is no doubt that, on the whole, service in the coastal batteries was monotonous and confining. A man was entitled to one day of leave for every ten days on duty, but even this leave could be cancelled. In emergencies all ranks were recalled to duty and kept in the forts for an indefinite period. This was so in December 1941 after Japan had declared war on Britain and the United States. While civilians hastily strung up blackout curtains and painted their car headlamps blue - which resulted in night-time collisions - the soldiers wore helmets, carried gas respirators and awaited an attack. Fire-fighting equipment was assembled, though it rarely consisted of more than buckets of sand and stirrup pumps for water. A similar crisis arose in June 1942 when Japan attacked the Aleutian Islands and Japanese submarines were active on the west coast. They torpedoed an American freighter on the 7th off nearby Cape Flattery. On the night of June 20th a sub shelled Estevan Point lighthouse on Vancouver Island; Fort Stevens, Oregon, was bombarded on the following night. In September a submarine-launched airplane bombed Mount Emily in Oregon. These events and the shocking conquest of Hong Kong and Singapore make the evacuation of the Japanese-Canadians from the Pacific coast understandable though not excusable. The diversionary attacks close to home justified the role of the coastal gunners. The sense of immediate danger, however, soon passed and the possibility of Japanese attack became more remote after the battles of the Coral Sea and Midway that summer. Japan's navy had lost much of its offensive power.

Walter Harrington, who became an officer in the regular army found life as a gunner in the Vancouver defences "deadening." His father's service in the British and Canadian armies impelled him to come north in May 1940 from San Diego, California, to enlist in Canada's armed forces. Harrington's past association with the coast artillery of the American National Guard led him to the Bessborough Armouries. "I went in there," he remembers, "and asked the adjudant about getting into the field artillery. 'Oh yes,' he said, 'join us.' I should have known better. So I went and joined the 15th (Vancouver) Coast Brigade." He was attached to the 58th Heavy Battery and sent to Point Grey in June. The petty vexations that Walter Harrington endured as a gunner still rankle. "At Point Grey they gave me a bedspring with one-by-four boards and two-by-fours for legs and you made a box-like thing out of this and that was a bed. I just hammered the thing together. And we had straw palliasses (mattresses) and no pillow because the army didn't believe in pillows. The guys from here brought pillows from home. The army didn't have any sheets though the air force did."[14] It might be added that issue blankets were to be marked as government property to discourage theft or sale to civilians.

The dress regulations for soldiers on leave struck Harrington as being particularly insensitive. Until the new battledress became available to all ranks in the second half of 1940, recruits were given First World War uniforms consisting of a peaked forage cap, a flared tunic, and riding breeches with cloth puttees. Some of the old outfits disintegrated when they were unpacked. With this order of dress the gunners had to wear a leather bandolier for rifle ammunition. Why a gunner should wear such a thing mystified Harrington. "It had to be polished, but it was completely useless." The ruling of area headquarters on dress was contained in the 15th's Part I Orders for February 1940.[15]

DRESS-SOLDIERS ON PUBLIC STREETS
(a) It has been observed that soldiers on individual duty or when walking out, are appearing on the streets improperly dressed, i.e., without greatcoats, or wearing denim trousers or breeches, when their unit is known to be in possession of full supplies of serge clothing or battle dress.
(b) This creates the impression that soldiers are suffering from lack of proper clothing, when, as a matter of fact, the condition is due to the soldiers' negligence to dress properly.
(c) If the order of dress requires the wearing of a greatcoat, a greatcoat will be worn. If the uniform available to an Infantry unit, under present conditions, is breeches and puttees, a soldier of that unit will not be permitted out of barracks in denim trousers because he finds it less trouble than putting on the breeches and puttees.
(d) Under present conditions, when adequate supplies of new uniforms are not yet available, the above mentioned practice is particularly undesirable. Officers Commanding will, therefore, ensure that all soldiers, when outside of barrack areas, are properly dressed in such uniform as is available to them.

Subsequent orders charged the men with walking about with coats unbuttoned, hands in their pockets, and for "considerable slackness in saluting."

For the soldiers the dress problem was not so clear-cut. Walter Harrington received "an old cavalry greatcoat that went down to my ankles which I couldn't wear out (of barracks...). Now to go out on pass, however, they only had so many uniforms so we guys used to trade. You had to go out in battledress so when some fellows came back on pass, then you got a size that was, more or less, your fit and put that on and went out on pass. But you couldn't go out in civilian clothes; you had to go out in uniform. Some guy decided that everyone had to go out in boots and puttees.(...) It was kind of silly because when you were walking around on pass you were clomp, clomp, clomping around in those boots with all those hobnails. This was a problem because you couldn't dance and you couldn't go into somebody's house with your hobnailed boots on - it was crazy. The other thing was that they never provided any transportation so we had to make our own way from the fort down to the streetcar stop at Alma (four miles away)."

It was policy in the 15th Coast to rotate men within the defensive installations and, like many others, Walter Harrington did a six month stint on Yorke Island. There he experienced more of "what is known as 'chicken shit'." There was no regular leave policy coordinated with the vessels visiting the island. "From Vancouver there were boats going by, but not only that, there was a regular passenger boat calling in there once a week, then a water boat and a supply boat coming in (from Kelsey Bay where other steamships stopped), one on a Tuesday and one on Friday. It was absolutely ridiculous to not give people passes when you were that close to home, - something like eighty percent of the men came out from Vancouver, married men, men with families - absolutely none of them could go. They were afraid they might not get back in time and (...) we had to be in the front line.'"

Most of those who had volunteered for service with the regular army had done so with the hope of going overseas and seeing some action. Harrington was no exception; he was marking time in the coastal defences. "The thing that kept us going," he says, "was the prospect of getting out of Canada. (...) A very good friend of mine went down to Arnprior - his home - and a friend of his mother was raising the 24th Anti-Tank Battery out of Toronto. And so he went up to Camp Petawawa and saw him and got a draft for himself and he asked that I be requested. So I got requested to join the 24th Anti-Tank Battery;

that's how I got out. I went overseas in October 1941, which is what I had joined to do." He remembers four others who came up from the United States and joined the 15th Coast. Three stayed for only two or three weeks; "they couldn't hack it and they deserted."

CHAPTER 8

Recessional

In the last two years of the Second World War, service in the Vancouver defences was more comfortable and less restrictive than it had been at the beginning of the conflict. For one thing, men were allowed out on pass in civilian clothes and, something that was even better, girls of the Canadian Women's Army Corps were attached to the local military units. The gradual change in mood is reflected in the war diaries of the 15th Coast. In 1939 the entries were a perfunctory account of personnel changes with only the slightest hint at the drama and hardships of the times:[1]

Vancouver, B.C.   2/9/39 1530   *Instructions to mobilize H.Q., 31st, 58th, and 85th Heavy Batteries received at Bde. H.Q. Documents and necessaries not available. Batteries manning War stations as follows: 31st Battery: 4 Officers and 47 O.R.'s (other ranks) at Stanley Park, 1 Officer and 5 O.R.'s at Narrows North, 58th Bty. 5 Officers and 46 O.R.'s at Bessborough Armouries pending construction of Point Grey Defences. 85th Bty. 3 Officers and 50 O.R.'s at York (sic) Island. (...)*

         10/9/39   *Mob. (mobilization) Plus 7. No documents or necessaries. Bde. H.Q.: 7 Officers and 21 O.R.'s at Bessborough Armouries. (...)*

         1500   *Message received from Area H.Q. Canada at State of War with Germany. (...)*

         15/9/39   *Mob. plus 11. Documentation continues. No changes in strength (now 347 all ranks) or disposition. Court of Enquiry re Bdr. Bajus held at Wireless station, Point Grey, evidence taken and adjourned until 16/9/39.*

Young Norm Bajus, whose death is neither noted nor explained in the diary, was killed in a most tragic accident. He was in the Point Grey guard-house where a permanent force soldier was demonstrating rifle drill. The instructor put down his own weapon, turned about, and, by error, resumed the lesson with a sentry's rifle. He did not know that there was a round in the chamber and, when he went through the challenge procedure, he pulled the trigger. Bajus received the bullet in the chest and fell down dead.[2] Six men of the Vancouver-Yorke Island defences died violently: three drowned and two were suicides. The one who killed himself in Vancouver did so at Stanley Park in the autumn of 1941. The soldier had beaten up a man he had found in his girlfriend's apartment. When she gave him the choice of apologizing to the victim or of never seeing her again, he decided to shoot himself. In the concrete "O-Pip" which housed the searchlight directing station and battery command post as well as the signals room where he was on duty, he propped a rifle against the wall and, by pressing the trigger with a stick, shot himself through the heart.[3] Such are the stories, like that of the **Fort Rae**, that were omitted in the war diary.

In 1942 when each Vancouver installation was allowed to keep its own diary, apart from that of the headquarters, a few novel details crept into the record. The diary keeper, however, still relied heavily on current weather and the standard phrase "Normal routine for training, duties and fatigues" to fill the pages. Witness these first entries for Point Grey in July 1942:[4]

Point Grey	1942	
Fort	6-7	*Weather: Clear and hot, Visibility good.*
		Normal training, duties and fatigues.
		0745 Col. (W.C.) Thackeray, C.R.C.A., Lt-Col. Sherman, D.O.M.E., Lt-Col. Hood, C.O. 15th (Van) Coast Reg't, Lt-Col. W.H.G. Lambert, C.O. (28th) A/A Reg't., inspected the Fort.
	7-7	*Weather: Overcast with rain. Visibility Poor.*
		Normal training duties and fatigues.
		0830 LtCol. Appleyard, R.M., and two of his staff arrived to mount the test 2-pdr. Naval Gun mounting. Gun mounted (...)
	9-7	*Weather: Overcast with rain, Visibility poor to fair.*
		Normal routine, duties and fatigues.
		1000 Naval Gun 2-pdr. # S2231 fired 74 Rounds under the supervision of Lt-Col. Appleyard, R.M. Present was Mr. J. Pearce and a party from the Dominion Bridge Co. Ltd.
		1515 2-Stopping rounds fired.
		1800 Lieut. E.H. Oswell, R.C.A. CA., transferred to Narrows North.
		2240 Lt-Col. A.O. Hood, C.O., visited the Fort. General Alarm practice. (...)
	13-7	*Weather: Visibility Good.*
		Name of 15th (Van) Coast Bde. R.C.A. CA. officially changed to 15th (Van) Coast Reg't. R.C.A. CA., and that of the 58th Heavy Battery, R.C.A. CA. to 58th Coast Battery, R.C.A. CA. under General Order No. 249/42.
		1730 4-Series-100 Rounds. 1" Aiming Shoot. Officers taking part: Major J.H. Bricker, Lieut, L.L. McKay, Lieut. E. Green, Lieut. H. Freeman. Visitors: Lieut-Col. A.O. Hood (...), Capt. A.C.

	Setterfield, D.O. and Capt. H.H. Colewell. Capt. T.L. Harrison reported for duty.
27-7	Work commenced on new buildings. (...)
	Weather: Visibility good.
	1135 Report received that Sub. spotted by plane at N.49° W.123°. Lookouts warned.

The burden of Vancouver's defence fell increasingly on the Point Grey fort and the 58th Coast Battery. Plans to add a rapid-firing, twin barrel 6-pounder gun on the south side of the First Narrows were shelved and the existing installations were gradually reduced. After August 1943 there was only a skeleton detachment at Stanley Park to maintain the guns. Under the reduced examination service, Narrows North was only to challenge large ships and naval vessels that had not been cleared by the one remaining patrol boat. The Steveston battery was taken out of action in January 1944; one of its 18-pounders had already been replaced by two 25-pounder gun/howitzers that gave mobile protection to the Sea Island airport and the rest of the Fraser delta. These modern guns were moved to Point Grey. In January 1942, just after the surprise attack on Pearl Harbor, a site at Wadsley on the north shore had been acquired for a Fire Command Post. This centre was equipped to coordinate all the guns and searchlights of the Vancouver defences against a naval attack. It had a panoramic view of the harbour and the Strait of Georgia. Fire command was transferred to Point Grey in 1944 and nothing remains of the F.C. Post in what is now McKechnie Park except the concrete base of the rangefinder.

On March 1st, 1944, the 58th and 85th became Independent Coast Batteries. Freed of close surveillance, the author of the 58th's war diary became less formal and, on occasion, humourous. Here are some sample entries:[5]

Vancouver, B.C.	1944 March		
		1	Effective 1 Mar. 44, 58th Coast Battery, R.C.A. becomes an independent Battery, H.Q. 15 (Van) Cst Regt RCA and 31 Cst Bty RCA being disbanded as of 29 Feb. 44. 58 Cst Bty RCA now, under command of Major H.W. Selbie, with Battery Headquarters and one Section at Point Grey Fort, also one section in each of the following forts, Narrows North and Point Atkinson, all of which are situated at Vancouver, B.C.
			58 Cst Bty RCA comes directly under H.Q. Vancouver Defences in all matters concerning training, administration, etc. Strength of Battery as of this date: 8 Officers - 284 other ranks. (...)
		7	Capt. F.C. Whitehead proceeds to Point Atkinson Fort from Point Grey Fort, and assumes command of Point Atkinson Fort, vice Capt. P.A.T. Ellis (o.c. Narrows North). Smoke Bomb let off at Point Grey Fort provides some excitement for Fire Piquet on duty. (...)
		13	Capt Cunningham and Capt McKiel of N.D.H.Q. visited Point Grey Fort re Proposed Radar O.P. site. (...)
			Dominion Bridge Company tested 2 pdr. equipment at Point Grey Fort (...)
		14	Inspector-General, Major-General J.P. McKenzie, and Staff, including Major Bartlett, Capt Hassell and Capt G. Rhodes of H.Q. Vancouver Defences, inspected Point Grey Fort from 1330 hours to 1600

hours this date. This was a very thorough inspection, and, surprisingly, very satisfactory (also very dry). In the evening personnel of Point Grey Fort played host to a party of C.W.A.C. (Canadian Women's Army Corps) personnel at a dance held in the Men's Canteen (approximately 40 CWAC personnel attending.) The girls voiced their appreciation and asked for a repetition. The Commanding Officer definitely approved of this. (...)

23 Major H.W. Selbie visited Narrows North and Point Atkinson Forts this date. Much damage has been done to camouflage by recent gales; all nets and dummy positions (to deceive enemy aircraft) need repair and replacements.
A very successful party (concert) was held at Point Grey Fort in the evening by the Blues Chasers; all ranks are very well inclined to agree that Fort life isn't so dreary, after all. (...)

25 Farewell party held at Point Grey Fort Officers' Mess for Lt-Col. C.K. Rosebrugh, late Commanding Officer of 15 (Van) Cst Regt RCA., who proceeds to assume command of 17 (NBC) (North B.C.) Coast Regt RCA at Prince Rupert, B.C. on 27 Mar. 44. (...)

26 C. of E. (Anglican) Church Parade held at Point Grey Fort, H/Capt. E. Linfoot officiating. R.C. Church Parades held at Narrows North and Point Atkinson Forts. (...)

27 Very poor American propaganda film shown at Point Grey Fort this evening. Personnel of this Unit do not appreciate films of this type. (...)

April
10 Draft of six (6) other ranks (practically all remaining active personnel of suitable age and Pulhems [physically fit] for overseas service with exception of N.C.O's.) proceed to Wetaskiwin, Alta., on 8th Input, 1 Cdn. Trg (training) Bde, 1915 hours this date. (...)

14 All barrack stores removed from Steveston Fort this date, with exception of that necessary for two O.R. caretakers (...)

19 Padre's Hour inaugurated this date (...) Concert entitled 'V for Vaudeville' held at Point Grey Fort in evening, which was very enjoyable. (...)

24 6th Victory Load Drive commenced this date; results for day fair. (...)

May
5 Interviews for N.C.O.'s eligible for reversion for Overseas service. (...)

8 Motion Picture entitled 'Lost Horizon' shown at Point Grey Fort this evening. (...)

9 Training Films shown during day. Gunners show a great deal of interest in these films. (...)

18 Battery Commander's Parade held at Point Grey Fort, at which the best dressed and equipped man was awarded a 48 hour pass. Much competition over this. (...)

19 43rd A.A. Bty conducted a 3.7" shoot in Fort area. (parachute flares were used as night-time targets)

	20	*General Alarm sounded at 1015 hours this date, on the report that a submarine had been sighted in Active Pass, proceeding South East. The All Clear was received at 1137 hours. Strength: 10 Officers, 265 Other Ranks. (...)*
June	7	*A special V.D. Film was shown at Point Grey Fort this date, with lecture by Capt. M.L. Edgar, RCAMC, Unit Medical Officer. (There had been "Private Consultations with Medical Officer" on May 26th.)*
	8	*Weather - warm; visibility - good.*

A special Garrison Parade was held at Connaught Park at 0900 hours to-day, in honour of the King's Birthday, His Majesty King George VI. Some 1800 troops took part in the parade. 58 Cst Bty RCA as expected, acquitted themselves very well under the command of Major C.H. Munsie, Capt. M.O.F. Cartwright being 2 i/c. Following the March Past, an address was given by His Honour, Lieut-Governor W.C. Woodward, Lieut-Governor of British Columbia.

Following the parade Sunday routine was in effect.

In the afternoon a Swimming Parade was held to Spanish Banks, under Lieut. J.E.E. Osborne.

In the evening a motion picture was shown at Point Grey Fort, in Men's Canteen. (...)

August		
	7	*Troops being moved to Point Grey Fort from Narrows North and Point Atkinson in preparation for York (sic) Island changeover. (60 O.Rs. were dispatched on the 15th) (...)*
18	0400	*First Party of 49 O.Rs. arrive at Vancouver from York Island, very grateful to see civilization again. (...)*
	2100	*Second Party of 60 O.Rs. left Vancouver for York Island; all men present and seemingly happy to be off.*

It is evident from these extracts that the officers were using the carrot as much as the stick to motivate the private soldiers. The officers were no longer dealing with the keen volunteers of 1939 who would accept discomfort with a small amount of grumbling. Nelson Darling, who was regimental adjutant from December 1939 to June 1941, said of those first years "morale was excellent, subject to the usual problem of disciplining Canadians."[6] By 1944 most of the original members of the 15th Coast Brigade had gone overseas. Some were held back by health or family ties and a good number of experienced officers and NCO's were deliberately retained as a reliable core for training recruits. The untrained recruits who replaced those gunners who had left were increasingly conscripts and not volunteers. They had been summoned to military service for home defence under the National Resources Mobilization Act (N.R.M.A.) of June 1940. They were very different from those men who had been in Vancouver's pre-war militia.

Before mobilization, according to Nelson Darling, the 15th Coast drew heavily on the Canadian-born population of British stock. If we can judge from the nominal roll of the 1st Searchlight Regiment in January 1940, the same was true of this unit. The vast majority of the 204 persons listed had English, Scottish or Irish surnames. The balance, eighteen men, had Germanic, French or Scandinavian names.[7] The author knows from acquaintance that more than half of these were English-speaking Canadians and not recent immigrants. Surnames are not a perfect indicator of peoples' cultural ties. They do indicate that the militia artillery of the Lower Mainland at the beginning of the Second World War had the same ethnic makeup as Vancouver's first militia units. The officers still came from the same occupational group. In 1939 the officers of the 15th Coast Brigade were, according to Allan M. McGavin who was the first commander of Narrows North, "mostly businessmen." They included a lawyer, an insurance underwriter, a dentist, a shipping agent, a post office employee, some schoolteachers, and the officials of such commercial enterprises as a flour mill, a lumber yard and a timber company. The men in the lower ranks came from across the city: they were students, truck-drivers, policemen, employees of a storage company, metalworkers and sawmill workers, as well as a few of the unemployed who were given their streetcar fare to the armouries. "They were," says Nelson Darling, "either very young or very old, including a few hangovers from the First War." The gulf between the two age groups was soon filled by recruiting in the first months of the Second World War.

The conscripts who replaced the "active service" volunteers in the coastal forts of British Columbia were a more diverse group. 67 members of the lower ranks of the 58th Independent Coast Battery were listed in the unit's Part I Orders for August 11th, 1944. The 46 N.R.M.A. men can be identified by their six numeral serial numbers, the so-called "box-car numbers." The general service volunteers were predominantly of British origin as were the officers and senior NCO's. But so was the largest group among the conscripts. In order of prominence, the surnames of the home defence conscripts were British (18), Slavic (12), Germanic (6), Italian (4), Scandinavian (3) and French (2).[8] The new elements brought into the coast artillery by conscription were the Ukrainian and German-speaking men from the Prairies and others from ethnic minorities, such as the Italian-Canadians, in Central Canada. The reluctance of those of East European ancestry to enlist was understandable: they had unhappy memories of compulsory military service in the Russian and Austro-Hungarian empires. The men from the Prairies also came from farms where their labour was needed and where they were isolated from world events. Put simply, they were indifferent to the war. The religious as well as cultural diversity of the 58th Battery was reflected in the provision made in April 1944 for leave during the Jewish Passover. It is, on the other hand, remarkable that in a region with a large Oriental population, the 15th Coast Brigade contained only one Chinese-Canadian; he was a volunteer who became a sergeant.

Given the high percentage of involuntary soldiers in the coastal defences, we can see why so much attention was paid to their welfare and why the keeper of the war diary kept track of the mood of the troops. The population of Vancouver had traditionally provided special entertainment and comforts for the servicemen. In the downtown area volunteers ran the Georgia Dug-Out, a recreation and social centre for members of the armed forces. In 1944 there were two more similar institutions: the United Service Centre and the Blue Triangle Women's Centre. In the hotels and taverns the soldiers were more likely to get into fights. In December 1941 the Lions Gate Riding and Polo Club sponsored a Christmas party and tea for the dependents of all serving gunners. Throughout the war it was common for private groups to arrange dances and concerts for the local troops. The soldiers were also given free passes to radio shows and to the performances of such celebrities as Jack Benny. All of this was quite apart from the entertainment provided within the forts. The fort record book for Point Grey noted dances, social evenings, quizzes, and the showing of such films as "Crime Doctor" and "Meet Mr. Death." Outdoor sports and indoor games were always a part of camp life.

Despite all the efforts made to reconcile the soldiers to life in the Vancouver defences and to banish that threat to morale, boredom, a few men were discontented. The war diaries and routine orders bear witness to the discipline problems in the forts. Article 420 of the King's Regulations (Canada) against traitorous actions and incitement to mutiny was to be read out on parade once every three months. Malcontents usually took a less dramatic course: they overstayed their leave or deserted outright. Desertions occurred at the rate of nearly one a month. Court martials are reported in the diaries though the offence is usually not described. Convicted offenders were sent to the detention barracks at Little Mountain in Vancouver. Courts of inquiry were convened for lesser matters such as the loss or destruction of equipment - careless driving being a common fault - and for injuries. The wounds were customarily inflicted by "friendly" forces; in a rugby game with the sappers the gunners suffered several casualties when one of their number was suspected of deliberate dirty play. Certain downtown cafes and dance halls were declared to be out of bounds and one can speculate on the vices that awaited the unwary soldier in these locations. Veneral disease was certainly one of them and the army countered with education, prophylactics and medical treatment. At the local military hospital a physician asked an infected soldier to divulge the name of his contact so that she too might be treated. "Well Doc," the soldier replied, "it's like this: when you cut yourself with a saw, can you tell what tooth on the blade done it?"

Garrison duty was certainly more comfortable in 1943-1944 than it had been in the first years of the war and, strange as it might seem, the conscripts received better treatment from their officers and NCO's than from certain civilians. Old sweats who were no longer in the armed forces dismissed the conscripts as "feather-bed soldiers" and "Mackenzie-King's Commandos," implying that they were simply cowards. The contemptuous term for the N.R.M.A. men that was most often used by the public was "zombies." Zombies were a feature of contemporary horror films; they were corpses resurrected to function as soulless labourers by Voodoo magic. "Conchie" was the epithet applied to conscientious objectors who were excused from military service. Those in authority over the conscripts were more tolerant; they knew that abusive treatment would make their own job more difficult. Part of their job was to encourage the home defence troops to volunteer for service abroad.

After the Canadian army became involved in the Italian campaign in July 1943 the demand for reinforcements increased. The soldiers in Canada, replaced by N.R.M.A. men, helped to supplement the voluntary enlistments available as reinforcements. With the Allied invasion of Normandy in June 1944 these men were insufficient to replace the losses, especially in the infantry. Pressure grew to strip the home defences of all manpower, whether volunteer or not. Canada's allies had accepted conscription for overseas service and her insistence of having a volunteer army in Europe seemed unrealistic. The N.R.M.A. soldiers were especially valuable since most were already trained and could go into action at once. Those in the coast artillery had not only been instructed in gunnery - the Vancouver defences were an artillery school of sorts - but they were also trained in basic military skills, field tactics and the use of small arms. The gunners were to be able to defend themselves against enemy landing parties.

From 1943 onward the N.R.M.A. men were continually asked to "go active." Officers appealed to the conscripts to "see their duty" and to volunteer for unrestricted service. Volunteers wore a "general service" patch on the sleeve that distinguised them from home defence troops. The American propaganda film that offended the Point Grey gunners was likely a part of this campaign. In late June, after the Normandy landings, combat veterans spoke to the men at Point Grey. One was a former NCO of the 15th Coast who had served with the American paratroops in Italy; the other was an Australian major who related his war experiences in the Pacific. Harry Mangles, who served as an NCO in the Vancouver-Yorke Island forts throughout the war, believes that about half of the conscripts eventually converted to active service. Some of them, he recalls, were very good soldiers.

Even before the reluctant decision of the Mackenzie-King government in November 1944 to send 16,000 conscripts to Europe, the Vancouver forts were closed down to release the soldiers there for other duties. The 58th Coast Battery was to be reduced to "A maintenance basis" on September 1st and the month of August was spent in preparation for that event. The gun and searchlights were removed from Point Atkinson and the installations at Narrows North, Stanley Park and Point Grey were to be looked after by a twenty man maintenance crew. Fifty N.R.M.A. gunners were transferred to a field artillery regiment on the 22nd of August while the remainder of the men were interviewed by an army examiner, presumably to obtain a few more volunteers. On the 31st these men and the last members of the disbanded 28th Anti-Aircraft Regiment were sent to the district depot for re-allocation. All that remained of the former 15th Coast Regiment were the twenty caretakers in Vancouver and the 85th Independent Coast Battery on Yorke Island.

The surrender of Japan on August 14th, 1945 forced a decision on the fate of Vancouver's coastal defences. Narrows North was abandoned immediately. The guns at Stanley Park were removed in September 1945 and though most of the huts there were demolished, the army did not vacate Ferguson Point. The officer's mess became a residence for the district commander. The Vancouver Parks Board objected to this and demanded the removal of the fence and the restoration of the point as parkland. As a consequence, the gun emplacements were dynamited and buried in April 1948 and the old mess was handed over to be converted into a tearoom. The adjoining concrete O-Pip and powerhouse were demolished in 1963. At Narrows North the camp was levelled and, amid piles of sand and gravel in what is now the West Vancouver works yard, the concrete gantry still stands. Point Atkinson camp was retained for many years as a forest wardens training school. Here and at Siwash Rock are two, nearly complete searchlight emplacements.

At Point Grey, on land that was reserved in the nineteenth century for the protection of the harbour, are the extensive remains of what was Vancouver's largest and longest-used coastal fort. At the end of the war in 1945 the camp area was given to the University of British Columbia which added huts from Tofino air base to the existing buildings. Fort Camp, as the area was called, provided additional lecture halls and quarters for a student body that had trebled with the arrival of former members of the armed services as government-assisted students. The guns of the battery - No.3 seems to have been replaced - were maintained by the army for training the revived 15th Coast Regiment (Reserve), R.C.A. When that unit reverted to field artillery in February 1948 arrangements were made to remove the guns. This happened late in the year or in 1949. The succeeding 102nd Coast Regiment (Reserve) of Vancouver went to Victoria-Esquimalt to be instructed on the more modern guns there. This continued until the disbanding of the regiment in December 1954. Two years later the forts on Vancouver Island were closed down. In Britain and Canada coastal artillery was declared to be an obsolete form of defence.

The coastal batteries had been built to meet the threat of surface vessels that had to come within sight of their target to launch their shells and torpedoes. Radar had deprived the attacker of surprise, especially when the assault was to be made by something as large and slow as a conventional warship. There were now other means of inflicting damage on fixed installations that were less hazardous to the attacker. By the 1950's it was evident that swift and high-flying aircraft and guided missiles were a greater peril than capital ships. The danger of naval attacks on Canada's ports, which had dominated the thoughts of defence planners before 1939, proved to be slight in the Second World War. Moreover, the coastal batteries had not prevented enemy submarines from harassing Allied shipping close to our shores. Only the Navy and the Air Force could deal with this submerged menace. It was plain that, except where a narrow passage forced ships to pass on the water's surface close to shore, the era of coast artillery had ended.

On the Lower Mainland of British Columbia, it is possible to recapture that earlier period of military history on Point Grey. Though Fort Camp and the central position of the gun battery were levelled in 1973-1974 to make way for the new Museum of Anthropology, two gun positions and a powerhouse remain atop the point and another powerhouse and a pair of searchlight towers can be seen on the beach below the cliff. The public memory is short and these searchlight emplacements are commonly known as "the gun towers." This forgetfulness was even more evident in the early 1970's when, in planning for the museum, no thought was given to the history of the site. The gun positions were regarded as so much immoveable concrete and the architect planned to disguise the flanking positions outside the building as Chinese hill tombs in an Oriental garden. The disappearance of the last visible coast artillery emplacements in the Lower Mainland was prevented by a campaign that received the support of, among others, veterans' groups, the Vancouver Historical Society, and the grand old man of Canadian military history, Col. Charles P. Stacey. With the cooperation of the University of British Columbia, on whose campus the site is located, the pedestal of No. 1 Gun has been marked off and preserved as a memorial to the military history of Point Grey and to the gunners who defended Vancouver during the Second World War.

APPENDIX
BIBLIOGRAPHY
CHAPTER NOTES
INDEX

Appendix

MILITIA ARTILLERY UNITS OF THE LOWER MAINLAND, 1866 - 1949

* - now defunct

NEW WESTMINSTER

	Date of Organization
Seymour Artillery Company	16 June 1866
became	
Seymour Battery of Garrison Artillery	10 July 1874
became	
No.1 Battery, **British Columbia Provisional Regiment of Garrison Artillery** (renamed B.C. Brigade of Garrison Artillery on 7 May 1886)	12 Oct. 1883
became	
No.4 Company, **British Columbia Battalion of Garrison Artillery** (renamed **5th [British Columbia] Regiment, Canadian Artillery** on 28 Dec. 1895)	25 Aug. 1893
became	
* No.1 Company, Second Battalion, **5th (B.C.) Regiment**, C.A. (converted to the 6th Battalion, Rifles, on 20 July 1899)	1 July 1898

VANCOUVER[1]

* No.5 Company, **British Columbia Battalion of Garrison Artillery/5th (B.C.) Regiment**, C.A.	16 Jan. 1894
* No.6 Company, **5th (B.C.) Regiment**, C.A.	28 Dec. 1895
(both were renumbered as No.2 and 3 Companies of the Second Battalion of the 5th [B.C.] Regiment, C.A., on 29 Sept. 1896. The Second Battalion became the 6th Battalion, Rifles, on 20 July 1899)	
31st, 68th, and 85th Batteries; **15th Brigade,** Canadian Field Artillery (renamed **15th Field Brigade,** Canadian Artillery, on 1 July 1925; "Royal" was added to "Canadian Artillery" in 1935)	2 Feb. 1920
became	

1. Some batteries of the battalions or brigades with headquarters in Vancouver were located elsewhere on the Lower Mainland.

31st, 58th, 68th, and 85th Batteries; **15th (Vancouver) Coast Brigade**, Royal Canadian Artillery (renamed **15th Coast Regiment**, R.C.A., in April 1942; the 68th Battery and the attached 5th Medium Battery became the 9th and 11th Batteries of the 1st Anti-Aircraft Regiment, R.C.A., on 15 May 1939 (see below); the 58th Battery was renumbered the 158th in Oct. 1946 after seven months as the 159th)   7 April 1938

became

31st, 85th, and 158th Batteries; **15th Field Regiment**, R.C.A. (renamed **15th Field Artillery Regiment** on 12 April 1960; the 209th and 210th Batteries, formerly of the 43rd Medium Anti-Aircraft Regiment (see below), were added on 15 Oct. 1959; the 210th Battery was disbanded in 1965 and the 85th and 158th Batteries followed suit in 1970; the 209th Battery became the 68th Battery in the same year)   5 Feb. 1948

* 1st, 2nd, and 3rd Batteries: **1st Searchlight Regiment**, R.C.A. (formerly British Columbia Hussars; disbanded 1 April 1946)   15 May 1939

9th, 10th and 11th Batteries, **1st Anti-Aircraft Regiment**, R.C.A.   15 May 1939

became

* 209th, 210th, and 211th Batteries; **43rd Heavy Anti-Aircraft Regiment**, R.C.A (renamed the **43rd Medium Anti-Aircraft Regiment** on 18 Aug. 1955; absorbed by the 15th Field Regiment on 15 Oct. 1959)   1 April 1946

201st, 202nd, and 203rd Batteries; **39th (Reserve) Field Regiment**, R.C.A.   1 April 1942

became

* 201st, 202nd, and 203rd Batteries; **11th (Reserve) Anti-Aircraft Regiment**, R.C.A. (disbanded 31 March 1946)   13 Nov. 1943

* 193rd, 194th, and 195th Batteries; **65th Light Anti-Aircraft Regiment**, R.C.A. (formerly the Irish Fusiliers; reverted to infantry on 1 Sept. 1958)   1 April 1946

7th Anti-Aircraft Gun Operations Room, R.C.A (made up from the 1st and 2nd (Reserve) Searchlight Batteries; this unit was disbanded on 30 Sept. 1957)   1 April 1946

Vancouver Coast Regiment, R.C.A.   1 July 1949

became

102nd Coast Regiment, R.C.A. (absorbed by the 43rd Heavy Anti-Aircraft Regiment on 31 Dec. 1954)   29 Sept. 1949

Bibliography

BIBLIOGRAPHY OF ARTICLES AND BOOKS RELATING DIRECTLY TO THE SUBJECT

Aikman, Bill & D. Cossette. "The Attack on Estevan Lighthouse," **The Sentinel,** Vol.X (1974), No.7, pp.11-14.

Beeston, C.G. "The 15th Field Brigade, Canadian Artillery: A History and Commentary - 1919-1933," **Canadian Defence Quarterly** (C.D.Q.), Vol.XV, No.4 (July 1938), pp.442-459.

Gough, Barry M. **The Royal Navy and the Northwest Coast of North America, 1810-1914** (Vancouver, 1971).

Great Britain, Privy Council: 1906, The Attorney-General of British Columbia versus The Attorney-General of Canada. 2 vols. (London, 1906), - This is popularly known as the "Deadman's Island Record" and includes maps of the government land reserves established in the Lower Mainland.

Harker, Douglas E. **The Dukes: the story of the men who have served in Peace and War with the British Columbia Regiment (D.C.O.), 1883-1973** (Vancouver, 1974).

Hogg, Ian V. **Coast Defences of England and Wales, 1856-1956** (Newton Abbot, 1974).

Hunter, T.M. "Coast Defence in British Columbia, 1939-1941: Attitudes and Realities," **B.C. Studes,** No.28 (Winter 1975-76), pp.3-28.

Letson, H.F.G. "Problems of Defence on the Pacific," C.D.Q., Vol.XV, No.4 (July 1938), pp.423-429.

Lower, A.R.M. "The Defence of the West Coast," C.D.Q., Vol.XVI, No.1 (Oct. 1938), pp.32-38.

Matthews, J.S. "This is Twentieth Anniversary of Formation of Vancouver's First Corps," **Vancouver Daily Province,** 17 Jan. 1914.

Matthews, J.S. and others. "Vancouver's Militia," **British Columbia Magazine,** June 1911, pp.551-557.

*Moogk, Peter N. "The Guns of Vancouver," Chuck Davis (ed.). **The Vancouver Book** (Vancouver, 1976), pp.210-212.

Moogk, Peter N. "The Long Watch for the War That Never Came," **U.B.C. Alumni Chronicle,** Vol.XXVIII, No.4 (Winter 1974), pp.28-29.

Nicholson, G.W.L. **The Gunners of Canada: The History of the Royal Regiment of Canadian Artillery.** 2 vols. (Toronto, 1967-72).

Rippengale, J.E. "The Story of Coastal Artillery in Victoria-Esquimalt," **Maritime Museum of British Columbia, Bulletin,** No.28 (March 1975), pp.1-5.

Robertson, F.A. 5th (B.C.) Regiment, Canadian Garrison Artillery (unpublished manuscript history, 1925).

Roy, Reginald H. "The Early Militia and Defence of British Columbia, 1871-1885," **British Columbia Historical Quarterly** (B.C.H.Q.), Vol.XVIII (1954), pp.1-28.

Silverman, Peter Guy. **A History of the Militia and Defences of British Columbia: 1871-1914** (M.A. thesis in History, University of British Columbia, 1956).

Stacey, Charles P. **Official History of the Canadian Army in the Second World War.** 3 vols. (Ottawa, 1967), Vol.I: **Six Years of War, The Army in Canada, Britain and the Pacific.**

Tucker, Gilbert N. "Canada's First Submarines: CC1 and CC2," B.C.H.Q., Vol.VII (1943) pp.147-170.

Tucker, Gilbert N. "The Career of H.M.C.S. 'Rainbow'," B.C.H.Q., Vol.VII (1943), pp.1-30.

Woodward, Frances M. "The Influence of the Royal Engineers on the Development of British Columbia," **B.C. Studies,** No.24 (Winter 1974-75), pp.3-51.

* A more detailed version of this article was published in **The Canadian Gunner,** Vol.XII (1976), pp.143-147.

Chapter Notes

CHAPTER 1

1. "Fenianism -- Our Situation," **British Columbian**, 16 June 1866; see also "Fenians and Fenianism" in **ibid.**, 20 June 1866.
2. "Defensive Measures," **British Columbian**, 16 June 1866.
3. "Formation of an Artillery Company," **British Columbian**, 16 June 1866.
4. "The Volunteer Movement," **British Columbian**, 20 June 1866.
5. "Volunteer Artillery Corps," **British Columbian**, 18 July 1866.
6. Col. P. Robertson-Ross, **Report on the State of the Militia of the Dominion of Canada for the Year 1872** (Ottawa, 1873), p.cxxvi.
7. Major-General E. Selby Smyth, quoted in Lieut. Col. F.A. Robertson, **5th (B.C.) Regiment Canadian Garrison Artillery**, unpublished manuscript history (Victoria, 1925,) chap. XIII, p.1. The author consulted the copy of this work held by Fort Rodd Hill Historic Park, Victoria B.C.
8. Robertson, chap.XIII, p.4.
9. Robertson, chap.XIII, p.4.
10. Robertson, chap.XIII, p.4.
11. C.F. Houghton in 1880, in Robertson, chap.XIII, p.7.
12. "The Queen's Birthday," **Mainland Guardian**, 28 May 1870. "Aunt Sally" reappeared in the May Day celebrations of 1873. The May Day festival at New Westminster had been sponsored, at least since 1871, by the Hyack Fire Fighting Company; not to be confused with the later Hyack Anvil Battery. **Hyack** is Chinook jargon for "hurry up."
13. "Queen's Birthday,...Meddling with the Battery," **Daily British Columbian**, 25 May 1883.
14. "Queen's Birthday," **Daily British Columbian**, 25 May 1883.
15. Lieut. Col. J.G. Holmes in 1886, in Robertson, chap. XVI, p.2.
16. Vancouver City Archives, J.S. Matthews Collection, Military Files, No. 12: B.C.B.G.A.
17. **Ibid.**, transcript of a letter from Lieut. Col. E.G. Prior to Capt. Townley, 1 May 1893, in which Prior explained the reasons for renumbering the companies and added "I think I know the feeling in N.W. well enough though to know it would be most unpopular as you are by far the oldest Co."
18. Frederick W. Howay & E.O. Scholefield, **British Columbia from the Earliest Times to the Present.** 4 vols. (Vancouver, 1914). Vol.III pp.68-71.
19. "The Number Changed," **Daily Columbian**, 26 August 1893.
20. "Trouble in the Artillery," **Daily Columbian**, 8 August 1894.
21. Robertson, chap.XVIII, p.15.
22. "Queen's Birthday," **Daily British Columbian**, 25 May 1889.
23. "Queen's Birthday," **Daily Columbian**, 25 May 1892.
24. "Queen's Birthday," **Daily Columbian**, 25 May 1893.

25. See, for example, Vancouver's **Daily News-Advertiser,** 26 May 1897 and 26 May 1899, which give 1865 as the foundation date of "the Most Ancient and Honorable Hyack Anvil Battery." The current assertion that the tradition began in 1871 is likely based on the Hyack **Fire Company's** sponsorship of the May Day celebrations which can be documented from this date. See footnote 12 on this matter.

CHAPTER 2

1. Fort Rodd Hill Reference Library, Ms. files, Military Reserves: Vancouver Area, re Point Grey Military Reserve, "The Crossman-Bourke Schedule."
2. Rudyard Kipling, **From Sea to Sea and Other Sketches.** 2 vols. (London, 1900), Vol.II, pp.55-57.
3. "Dominion Day," **Daily British Columbian,** 2 July 1889; see also "Vancouver Celebration," **ibid.,** 5 July 1887.
4. "Matters Military," **Daily World,** 12 June 1893.
5. "A New Battery of Garrison Artillery," **Daily News-Advertiser,** 7 July 1893; "Artillery for Vancouver," **Daily World,** 6 July 1893.
6. "A New Battery," **Daily News-Advertiser,** 7 July 1893.
7. "This is Twentieth Anniversary of Formation of Vancouver's First Corps," by Maximgun (J.S. Matthews), **Vancouver Daily Province,** 17 January 1914.
8. Vancouver City Archives, J.S. Matthews Collection, Military Files, No. 45: Armouries, Drill Halls, Rifles Ranges; Notes on the old "Imperial Opera House."
9. "Battery Parade," **Daily News-Advertiser,** 10 May 1894.
10. "Matters Military," **Daily News-Advertiser,** 24 May 1897.
11. Vancouver City Archives, J.S. Matthews Collection, Newspaper Dockets, Military, No. 22: B.C.B.G.A., newspaper article by William D. Newell, probably from the **Vancouver Daily Province** in the 1930's.
12. "This is Twentieth Anniversary," **Vancouver Daily Province,** 17 January 1914.
13. Vancouver City Archives, J.S. Matthews Collection, Military Files, No. 12: B.C.B.G.A., Transcribed letters from Lieut. Col. E.G. Prior to T.O. Townley, 1892-1895.
14. See footnote 11.
15. "Dominion Day," **Daily News-Advertiser,** 1 July 1899.
16. Quoted in Robertson, chap.XIX, p.5; author unable to locate original for verification and the quotation might come from another newspaper.
17. J.S. Matthews in 1924, quoted in Robertson, chap. XIX, p.5.
18. Quoted in Douglas E. Harker, **The Dukes: the story of the men who have served in Peace and War with the British Columbia Regiment (D.C.O.), 1883-1973** (Vancouver, 1974), p.22.
19. Quoted in Harker, p.23.
20. "Matters Military," **Daily News-Advertiser,** 6 August 1899.
21. "Banquet Proves That Old Soldiers Don't Fade Away," **Vancouver Daily Province,** 8 Feb. 1940. See also "Boys of Old Brigade," **ibid.,** 8 March 1937 and "Members of City's First Militia Meet," **ibid.,** 27 Jan. 1938.

CHAPTER 3

1. Quoted in Margaret A. Ormsby, **British Columbia: A History** (Toronto, 1958), p.378.
2. Gilbert Norman Tucker, The Career of H.M.C.S. 'Rainbow', **The British Columbia Historical Quarterly** (hereafter B.C.H.Q.), Vol VII (1943), p.7.
3. "Will Rainbow Stay As Coast's Sole Defence?," **Vancouver Daily Province**, 30 July 1914.
4. G.N. Tucker, "Canada's First Submarines: CC1 and CC2," B.C.H.Q., Vol. VII (1943), pp.153-154.
5. Letter of 10 December 1974 from C.H. Crickmay of Calgary to the **University of British Columbia Alumni Chronicle,** in whose Summer 1975 issue it was published. Additional personal information from a letter of 22 January 1975 from Mr. Crickmay to Peter Moogk.
6. Tucker, "The Career of H.M.C.S. 'Rainbow'", p.13.
7. Tucker, "The Career of H.M.C.S. 'Rainbow'," p.17.
8. "Wireless Warns Ships on Pacific," **Vancouver Daily Province,** 7 September 1914.
9. Public Archives of Canada, R.G. 24, Vol.II-907, File E26-744, Letter of Lieut. Arthur M. Saul of H.M.C. hospital ship Prince George to senior officer, Esquimalt; dated 20 August 1914.
10. "'Admiral Lucas' Tells How City Was Fortified During the War," by Arthur W. Mayse, **Vancouver Daily Province,** 15 January 1938.
11. "All Military Units in Province Are Called Out," **Vancouver Daily Province,** 11 August 1914.
12. "Reserve Gunners Form Battery," **Vancouver Daily Province,** 5 September 1914.
13. "Artillerymen On Parade," **Vancouver Daily Province,** 9 September 1914.
14. "Commandant Sees Gunners Work Out," **Vancouver Daily Province,** 11 September 1914.
15. "Local Brevities," **Vancouver Daily Province,** 17 September 1914.
16. "Keep The Wheels of Industry Here in Motion," **Vancouver Daily Province,** 9 September 1914.

CHAPTER 4

1. Quoted in G.W.L. Nicholson, **The Gunners of Canada.** 2 vols. (Toronto, 1967-72), Vol.II, p.3.
2. C.G. Beeston, "The 15th Field Brigade, Canadian Artillery: A History and Commentary - 1919-1933," **Canadian Defence Quarterly** (hereafter C.D.Q.), Vol.XV, No.4 (July 1938), pp.442-443.
3. Minutes, Reorganization of Militia Artillery in Vancouver, Vancouver, 16 July 1919, copy held by R.V. Stevenson.
4. **Ibid.**
5. Letter of Brigadier General A.G.L. McNaughton to Lieutenant Gordon Chutter, 9 January 1920, copy held by R.V. Stevenson.

6. Wyn Van der Schee, A register of regiments and batteries of The Royal Regiment of Canadian Artillery (unpublished typescript, 1976), Page 27.
7. Beeston, "The 15th Field Brigade," p.443.
8. Nicholson, **The Gunners,** II, p.23.
9. Beeston, "The 15th Field Brigade," p.444.
10. **Ibid.,** p.444.
11. **Ibid.,** p.445.
12. "Vancouver Battery Wins First Honours," **Vancouver Daily Province,** 24 Oct. 1922.
13. 15th Field Artillery Regiment Archives, Exercise Report by Major J.G. Chutter, 1928.
14. Memorandum of Association of the Vancouver Armoury Association Limited, 7 August 1928, copy held by R.V. Stevenson.
15. "Armoury is Named Bessborough," **Vancouver Daily Province,** 28 March 1933.
16. "New Armouries Are Opened by His Excellency," **Vancouver Daily Province,** 28 March 1934.
17. A.R.M. Lower, "The Defence of the West Coast," C.D.Q., Vol.XVI, No.1 (Oct. 1938), p.32.
18. H.F.G. Letson, "Problems of Defence on the Pacific," C.D.Q., Vol.XV, No. 4 (July 1938), pp.427-428.
19. Public Archives of Canada (hereafter P.A.C.), R.G. 24, Vol.2693, Summary of Forms and Scales of Attack on Vancouver, 1 February 1937.
20. P.A.C., R.G. 24, Vol.2693, file HQS 5199-C, Vol.I, Summary of Observations and Recommendations for the Defences of Vancouver, 1 February 1937.
21. "Beauty Takes the Count," **Vancouver Daily Province,** 9 February 1938.
22. "First Test of Stationary Guns Shows City Artillery's Skills," **Vancouver Daily Province,** 9 July 1938.
23. "A Nonchalant Government," **Vancouver Daily Province,** 31 May 1938.
24. "Big Air Defense for the City," **Vancouver Daily Province,** 15 June 1939.

CHAPTER 5

1. "Three Militia Units in City Are Mobilized," **Vancouver Daily Province,** 26 Aug. 1939.
2. Letter of T.M. Hunter, Associate Professor of History at Carleton University, to P.N. Moogk, 4 Feb. 1975.
3. Public Archives of Canada (hereafter P.A.C.), Point Grey B.C., Fort Record Book, Vol.II, Vancouver Fire Command Orders, 6 Oct. 1942, "Operations."
4. "Plane, Crash Boat in Rescue," **Vancouver Daily Province,** 3 Jan. 1940; "British Columbia's Ports Well Guarded by Royal Canadian Air Force," **ibid.,** 6 Jan. 1940; "Ex-Jericho Commander wants hangars saved," **ibid.,** 11 April 1977.
5. See footnote 3; "Description of the Fortress."
6. Letter of T.M. Hunter to the editor of the **U.B.C. Alumni Chronicle,** 11 Jan. 1975; reprinted in part in the Spring 1975 issue of the **Chronicle,** p.38.
7. "British Columbia Militia Units Swing Into Action," **Vancouver Daily Province,** 28 Aug. 1939; "B.C.'s Militia is Prepared," **ibid.,** 29 Aug. 1939; "Ears of Army Are Made

Here," **ibid.,** 13 Jan. 1940; Conversations with Nelson E. Longeuay, Lloyd Snider and Angus M. Tierney of the 1st Searchlight Regiment, 11 April 1975.

    8. "Stanley Park Guns Held Equal To Light Warships," **Vancouver Daily Province,** 7 Jan. 1939. Surviving officers of the 15th Coast Brigade are unable to identify the officer who was the reporter's informant.

    9. "The Way of the Sinner is Hard," **The Ubyssey,** 17 Oct. 1939; see also "Students Land in Garrison Guard-Room" in the same issue.

    10. See footnote 3; "Administration."

    11. P.A.C., War Diary, 15th (Vancouver) Coast Brigade, R.C.A., Vol.I, 29 Dec. 1939.

CHAPTER 6

    1. John T. Walbran, **British Columbia Coast Names** (Ottawa, 1909), pp.229, 537.
    2. **British Columbia Pilot** (Victoria, 1884).
    3. **British Columbia Pilot** (Victoria, 1905).
    4. "B.C. Island Now Defense Reserve," **Vancouver Daily Province,** 1 October 1938.
    5. Public Archives of Canada, R.G. 24, Vol.3967, File NSS 1047-7-5, Letter from Naval Headquarters at Esquimalt to Admiral Kingsmill, 12 October 1914.
    6. Royal Canadian Artillery Museum (C.F.B. Shilo), War Diary, 85th Heavy Battery, R.C.A., August 1939.
    7. R.C.A. Museum, War Diary, 85th Heavy Battery, May 1941.
    8. Conversation of Lieut. D. Dashwood-Jones with Major R.V. Stevenson, 11 August 1977.
    9. Conversation of Lt. Col. F.C. Garrett with R.V. Stevenson, 3 August 1977.
    10. Conversation with D. Dashwood-Jones, 11 August 1977.
    11. Conversation of Major C.A. Buchanan with R.V. Stevenson, 3 August 1977.
    12. Conversation with F.C. Garrett, 13 July 1977.
    13. The **New Yorker** (of Yorke Island), Vol.II, 26 March 1944.
    14. Conversation with F.C. Garrett, 3 August 1977.
    15. R.C.A. Museum, War Diary, 85th Coast Battery, R.C.A., June 1942.
    16. **Ibid.,** July 1942.
    17. Alan Greene, "Five Hundred Miles," **The Log,** New Series, Vol.XII (1944), Nos.1-2, p.2.
    18. R.C.A. Museum, War Diary, 85th Coast Battery, August 1945.

CHAPTER 7

    1. This point was raised by John Swettenham of the Canadian War Museum at the Canadian Historical Association meeting in June 1975 and is developed by T. Murray Hunter in "Coast Defence in British Columbia, 1939-1941: Attitudes and Realities," **B.C. Studies,** No. 28 (Winter 1975-76), pp.3-28.

    2. "Shore Batteries on West Coast Ready For All Enemy Raiders," **Vancouver News-Herald,** 18 May 1940.

3. Public Archives of Canada (hereafter P.A.C.), War Diary of the 15th (Vancouver) Coast Brigade, Vol.I, Copy of 20 Feb. 1940 letter from Major C.K. Rosebrugh to Area Headquarters and Point Grey Battery Commander's Report on Gun Practice Seawards on 14 and 15th Feb. 1940 joined to Part I Orders.

4. "Just Target Practice," **Vancouver Daily Province,** 15 Feb. 1940.

5. "Fifteenth (Vancouver) Coast Brigade Mans Guns Along the Dominion's Pacific Ramparts," **Vancouver Daily Province,** 27 June 1942.

6. P.A.C., Stanley Park, Fort Record Book, **Notice to Mariners/Port of Vancouver B.C./No.4 (15-12-41).** See also "New Naval Rules Govern Port," **Vancouver Daily Province,** 6 Sept. 1939, and "War-Time Rule Governs Ships," **ibid.,** 7 Sept. 1939.

7. 12 Aug. 1975 conversation with Victor R. Voisey of Cloverdale B.C., formerly of the 11th Anti-Aircraft Regiment, R.C.A.

8. "Ship Halted Here By Warning Shot," **Vancouver Daily Province,** 17 Feb. 1940; "Warning Shot Stops Vessel," **Vancouver Sun,** 17 Feb. 1940.

9. 22 April 1977 conversation with D. Kenneth Brown of Delta B.C.

10. Conversation with E.L. "Paddy" Copeland, forest ranger at Point Atkinson, in August 1974.

11. The entire story is reconstructed from information supplied by W.W. Blackhall, D. Kenneth Brown, E.L. Copeland, J.R. Holden, Digby Jones (son of W.G. Jones of the Burrard Dry Docks stores department), Alfred O. Hood, Allan M. McGavin, A.F. Menzies, H.H. "Porky" Pearson, Harry Mangles, and Percy Ridgeway-Wilson (President of the Court of Inquiry). The war diaries and the routine orders of the 15th Coast mention the court of inquiry but provide no account of the accident.

12. "Finest in Comfort and Food Is Provided for Soldiers In Dominion's New Army," **Vancouver Daily Province,** 18 June 1941.

13. "He's in the Army - and Gunner Pat Really Likes It," **Vancouver Sun,** 18 June 1941.

14. Conversations with Walter Harrington, 8 May 1975 and 1 Sept. 1977.

15. P.A.C., War Diary, 15th (Vancouver) Coast Brigade, Headquarters, Folder 1, File 6, Part I Orders for 8 Feb. 1940; see also those for 28 Feb. 1940.

CHAPTER 8

1. Public Archives of Canada (hereafter P.A.C.), War Diary, 15th (Vancouver) Coast Brigade, R.C.A., Vol.I, p.1.

2. The details of this story were provided by Al Clark, Arne Knudsen, and Harry Mangles, all former members of the 15th Coast.

3. Nelson Darling who, as adjutant, participated in the investigation of this suicide, furnished most of the details.

4. P.A.C., War Diary, 15th (Vancouver) Coast Brigade/Regiment, R.C.A., Vol.II, Point Grey subsection.

5. P.A.C., War Diary, 58th Independent Coast Battery, R.C.A., Vol.I.

6. Interview with Nelson Darling in May 1975.

7. Nominal roll of the 1st Searchlight Regiment, R.C.A., dated 1 Jan. 1940, in the possession of Nelson E. Longeuay of Port Alberni B.C.

8. P.A.C., War Diary, 58th Independent Coast Battery, Vol.I, Part 1 Orders, 11 Aug. 1944.

Index

Roman numerals = CHAPTERS
Arabic numerals = PAGES
n. = footnotes

Adams, Fred   V, 82
Adjutant - General of Militia   I, 15
Air Defences   IV, 60;   V, 63, 82, 83;
   VI, 91, 92
Albert Head   V, 61, 64
Alert States of Defences   V, 64
Aleutian Islands   VII, 101
Alexander, F.W.   II, 26
H.M.S. **Algerine**   III, 32, 50
H.M.C.S. **Allaverdy**   VI. 88:
Ambleside   VII, 99
Ammunition Problems   V, 84;   VI, 89
Anglo-British Columbia Packing Company
   III, 50;   VI, 87
Appleyard, R.M.   VIII, 105
H.M.C.S. **Armentieres**   IV, 59;   VI, 88, 89
Army Week, 1942   VII, 96
H.M.A.S. **Australia**   III, 50
Bainbridge, W.N.   III, 52
Bajus, Norman   VIII, 104
Bartlett, Major   VIII, 106
Beatty Street Armouries   II, 30
Beeston, Cyril G.   IV, 58
Bell-Irving, M.O.   III, 52
Bessborough Armouries   IV, 57-58;   V, 82;
   VI, 87;   VII, 101;   VIII, 104;
Black, Dr. W.S.   I, 14, 17
Blue Chasers   VIII, 107
Blue Triangle Women's Centre   VIII, 109
Boer War   II, 28
Bole, William Norman   I, 18-19
Bonson, Lieut.   I, 20
Boorman, H.E.   III, 52
Borden, Sir Robert   III, 32, 51
Border Prince, The   VI, 88, 90
Boult, G.A.   II, 25
Boultbee, F.W. "Tom"   II, 25
Bourke, Commander   II, 22
Bowden, William   I, 14
Boys, F.   II, 26
Bray, H.R.   IV, 58
Bren Guns   V, 63, 83
Bricker, J.H.   VIII, 105
British Columbia, Province of   I, 15, 16, 18;
   III, 31, 49; and **PASSIM**
British Columbia Battalion of Garrison Artillery,
   I, 19; II, 24   see also 5th (British
   Columbia)
British Columbia Hussars (Armoured Car)
   IV, 60
British Columbia Provisional Regiment (or Brigade) of Garrison Artillery   I, 18
British Columbian Newspaper   I, 13-15, 18

British Empire,   II, 25;   IV, 59
Brown, D. Kenneth   VII, 99-100
Brown, Ebenezer   I, 15
Buie, John   I, 21
Burrard, Lieut.   VI, 86
Burrard Dry Dock Co. Ltd.   VII, 100
Burrard Inlet   I, 15, 18;   II, 22-24;   V, 62;
   and **PASSIM**
"C" Battery, C.A.   II, 25
Cambie Street Grounds   II, 28
Canadian Artillery Association   IV, 57
Canadian Expeditionary Force   IV, 54
Canadian Fusiliers Regiment   VI, 90
Canadian Pacific Railway   I, 18;   II, 22, 24;
   IV, 57
Canadian Scottish Regiment   VI, 90
Canadian Women's Army Corps   VIII, 104, 107
Cape Coronel, Battle of   III, 53
Cape Flattery   VII, 101
Capilano River   V, 62
Cartwright, M.O.F.   VIII, 108
Caulfeild Cove   VII, 99
Cavanagh, The   VI, 88
Central Park Rifle Range   II, 27
Chester, George   V, 82
Chile   III, 49, 53
Church Parades   VIII, 107
Chutter, J.G.   IV, 57, 58
Clough, John   II, 26
Coast Artillery as a form of defence   VIII, 111,
   112;
Coast Artillery Searchlights   IV, 60;
   V, 62; VI, 87, 89, 91, 92;
   VII, 106, 111;
Cobourg Heavy Battery, C.A.   III, 51, 52
Coghlan, F.T.   IV, 55
Colewell, H.H.   VIII, 106
Columbia Detachment of the Royal Engineers,
   I, 12
Columbian Newspaper   VI, 92
Committee of Militia Reorganization (Otter
   Committee)   IV, 54
H.M.C.S. **Comox**   VI, 87
Connaught, Duke of   I, 20;   II, 30
Conscripts or N.R.M.A. Men   VIII, 109,
   110, 111
Copeland, E.L.   VII, 99
Coral Sea   VII, 101
Cornish, J.C.   II, 26
Cowan, Robert   I, 14
Crease, Henry P. Pellew   I, 14, 15
Crickmay, Colin H.   III, 50
Crossley, Gordon Y.L.   IV, 60;   VI, 87;
   VII, 95-96
Crossman, Col.   II, 22
Crossman-Bourke Schedule   II, 22
Cummins, Allan   I, 14
Cutch, The   II, 26
Daily Columbian Newspaper   I, 20
Daily World Newspaper   II, 25

124

Darling, Nelson   VIII, 108, 109
Davy Jones, The   VI, 86
Daykin, A.N.   III, 52
Deaths in Vancouver Defences   VIII, 104, 105
Department of Militia (Canada)   I, 15, 20;
   II, 24;   IV, 55
Department of National Defence   IV, 59
Deputy Adjutant-General   I, 18
Desertions   VII, 101;   VIII, 110
Diggle, Commander   VI, 86
Dominion Bridge Co. Ltd.   VIII, 105, 106
Dominion Day Celebrations   I, 17;   II, 24, 25, 27;   IV, 60
Dominion of Canada, Government of   I, 16; and **PASSIM**
Douglas, Sir James   I, 12, 13
Dresden, The   III, 53
Duff-Stuart, J.   II, 26
Dummy Guns   II, 27;   IV, 59;   VIII, 107
DuMoulin, R. Theo.   V, 61;   VI, 91
   VII, 94-95
Dutch Harbour   VI, 92
Earl of Bessborough   IV, 58
Earl of Stradbrook Cup   IV, 57
Edgar, M.L.   VIII, 108
18-Pounder Guns   IV, 57, 60;   V, 63, 84
   VII, 98;   VIII, 106
85th Battery, C.F.A. (1918-19)   III, 53
85th Battery, C.F.A. (1920-38)   IV, 55
85th Heavy Battery, R.C.A. (1938-45)   V, 61;
   VI, 87;   VIII, 104, 106
11th Irish Fusiliers   II, 30
11th Light Anti-Aircraft Regiment (Reserve),
   R.C.A.   photo
Ellis, P.A.T.   VIII, 106
Emden, The   III, 31
Enlistment for Overseas Service   VIII, 110
Esquimalt   I, 15, 17;   II, 24, 25, 28;   III, 32,
   49, 51;   IV, 59, 60;   V, 61;   VI, 86, 87
Estevan Point Lighthouse   VI, 92;   VII, 101
Ethnic Composition of Militia   II, 25
Ethnic Composition of Coast Artillery During
   Second World War   VIII, 108, 109
Evacuation of Japanese-Canadians in 1942
   VII, 101
Examination Line   VII, 98
Examination Service   III, 49;   VI, 88;
   VII, 96-98;   VIII, 106;
Examination Vessels (X-Vics)   VI, 88;
   VII, 96-9;
Falkland Islands, Battle of   III, 53
Fanning Island   III, 50
Fenians   I, 13, 14
Ferguson Point Battery   IV, 59;   V, 83;
   VI, 91;   VII, 98;   VIII, 111;
Field Ambulance (18th)   II, 30
5th "British Columbia" Regiment, C.A.   I, 20;
   II, 28, 29
5th (B.C.) Coast Brigade, R.C.A.   V, 61;
   VII, 96

5th Company, B.C.B.G.A.   II, 24, 25
5th Heavy Battery, R.C.A.   VI, 87
5th Medium Battery C.A.   IV, 57, 60
5th Siege Battery, C.A.   IV, 55
15th Brigade, C.F.A. (1916-18)   III, 52;
   (1920-38), IV, 55, 57
15th Field Brigade, R.C.A.   IV, 57, 58, 59, 60;
15th (Vancouver) Coast Brigade Regiment,
   R.C.A.   IV, 60;   V, 61, 84;   VI, 87;
   VII, 96, 101, 102;   VIII, 105, 108, 111
58th Battery, C.F.A.   IV, 55
58th Heavy Battery, R.C.A.   V, 61, 84;
   VI, 90;   VII, 96, 102;   VIII, 104, 105, 106, 108, 111
Films shown to Gunners   VII, 107, 109
Fire Commander's Orders of 1942   V, 62
Fire Command Post   V, 64;   VIII, 106
1st Anti-Aircraft Regiment, R.C.A.   IV, 60;
   V, 84
1st Searchlight Regiment, R.C.A.   IV, 60;
   V, 61, 82, 84;   VIII, 109
First Narrows   II, 22;   IV, 59;   V, 61;
   VII, 98;   VIII, 105
First World War   III, 31 and **PASSIM**
Fishermen's Reserve   VI, 88
Flanders   III, 53
Fleming, Sir Sanford   III, 50
Food of Troops   VII, 100,
Forin, John Andrew   I, 20
Forms of attack expected in 1937   IV, 59
4-inch Guns   III, 51;
4.7-inch Coastal Guns   V, 63, 64, 82;
   VI, 87, 88, 89, 92;
Fort Langley   I, 12
Fort Macaulay   IV, 59
Fort McNab (Halifax)   V, 65
Fort Rae, The   VII, 99;   VIII, 105
Fort Stevens, Oregon   VII, 101
40-mm Bofors, Light Anti-Aircraft Guns   V, 83;
   VI, 92;
43rd Anti-Aircraft Battery, R.C.A.   VIII, 107
France   III, 53
Fraser River   I, 12
Freeman, H.   VIII, 105
Gardner-Johnson, Charles   II, 24
Garrett, F.C.   VI, 90
General Mackenzie, The   VI, 93
George V, H.M. King   II, 29
George the dog   VI, 90
Georgia dug-out   VIII, 110
Georgie, The   VII, 98
Germany   V, 61, 82;   VI, 87;   VIII, 104
Governor-General's Cup   IV, 57
Grant Challenge Cup   IV, 57
Green, E.   VIII, 105
Greene, Alan D.   VI, 92
Guernsey, F.W.   VI, 87
Gun Drill   I, 17;   II, 26;   IV, 59
Gun Shed at Vancouver   II, 26

Halifax, N.S.   V, 82;   VI, 87, 88
Hand, George   I, 14
Hardwicke Island   VI, 85, 86, 89
Harrington, Walter   VII, 101-103
Harrison, T.L.   VIII, 106
Hassell, Capt.   VIII, 106
Hastings Park   IV, 56
H.M.S. **Hecate**   VI, 85
Hicks, Ken W.   V, 83
Holden, J.R.   VII, 100
Holly Leaf, The   III, 50;   VI, 87
Holmes, G.W.   I, 14
Home Defence Troops   VI, 90, 92
Home Guard of Vancouver   III, 52
Home Guards of New Westminster   I, 13, 14
Hong Kong   VI, 90;   VII, 101
Hood, Alfred O.   VII, 96, 99,   VIII, 105
Horses for Militia   VI, 55, 56
Horse Show Building   IV, 56, 57
Hose, Walter   III, 50;   VI, 86
Hotel Georgia   IV, 58
Houghton, Charles Frederick   I, 16, 17
Howitzers of New Westminster Battery   I, 15, 16, 17, 18, 20
Hudson's Bay Company   I, 12
Hunter, T. Murray   V, 61, 82
Hurdman Challenge Cup   IV, 57
Hyack Anvil Battery, See most Ancient and Honourable Hyack Anvil Battery
Hyack Fire Fighting Company   I, 20
Imperial Opera House   II, 25
Ivy Leaf, The   III, 50;   VI, 87
IZUMO, The   III, 50
Jamieson, James W.   VII, 98
Japan   III, 50;   IV, 58, 59;   VI, 93;   VII, 98, 101;   VIII, 111
Jericho Beach Air Station   V, 64;
Jericho Naval Reserve   II, 22
John Antle, The   VI, 92
Johnson, Lacey C.   II, 24, 27
Johnstone Strait   V, 63;   VI, 85
Joint Staff Committee   IV, 59
Juan de Fuca Strait   V, 63
Kelsey Bay   VI, 85;   VII, 102
King's Birthday   IV, 60;   VIII, 108
Kipling, Rudyard   II, 23
Kitsilano   IV, 58
Knights of Labour   II, 23
Knudsen, Arne P.   VII, 100
Komagata Maru, The   III, 32
Labranche, Napoleon   II, 25
Lambert, W.H.G.   VIII, 105
Laurel Leaf, The   III, 50;   VI, 87
Laurier, Sir Wilfred   III, 50
Leipzig, The   III, 31, 50, 53
Lessons of Mobilization in 1939   V, 84
Letson, H.F.G.   IV, 59;   VI, 87
Lewis Machine Guns   V, 83;   VI, 91;
Liliuokalani, Queen   II, 23
Lindsay, James   I, 14

Linfoot, E.   VIII, 107
Linn, John   I, 14
Lions Gate Bridge   IV, 59;   V, 62, 84;   VII, 99
Little Mountain Detention Camp   VIII, 109
Logan, W.H.   III, 49
Lorne, Marquis of, and H.R.H. Princess Louise   I, 18
Lower, A.R.M.   IV, 58
Lucas, Eddie A.   III, 51
Macaulay Plains   II, 27
Macaulay Point   II, 27
McBride, Sir Richard   III, 49
McCullock, David   I, 14
MacDonald Challenge Trophy   IV, 57
Macdougall, A.G.   VI, 93
McGavin, Allan M.   VIII, 109
Mackay, A.C.N.   III, 52
Mackay, L.L.   VIII, 105
McKay, Major   III, 52
McKechnie Park   VIII, 106
McKenzie, J.P.   VIII, 106
Mackenzie-King, W.L.   IV, 56;   VIII, 111
McNaughten, Lieut.   I, 18
McNaughten, A.G.L.   IV, 55
Mainland Gaurdian Newspaper   I, 17
Malcolm Island   VI, 86
Mangles, Harry   VIII, 111
Marrion, R. Frank   II, 26, 27
Martin, L.A.   II, 25
Martin, Lionel   V, 84
Martini-Henry Rifles   II, 24
Mason, Don   VII, 100
Matthews, James Skitt   I, 19;   II, 25, 26
Mayse, Arthur   III, 51
Mechanized Artillery   IV, 57;
Menzies, A.F.   VII, 100
Mexico   III, 31
Midway, Battle of   VII, 101
Military and Naval Reserves   II, 22
Milne, G.E.   III, 52
Minister of Militia   I, 19
Mobilization in 1939   V, 61, 84
Mock, Lieut.   III, 51
Moody, Richard Clement   I, 12;   II, 22
Morale   VII, 100;   VIII, 108
Most Ancient and Honourable Hyack Anvil Battery   I, 21
Mount Emily, Oregon   VII, 101
Mowat, Lieut.   I, 18, 20   II, 23
Munsie, C.H.   VIII, 108
Murray, John   I, 14
Museum of Anthropology   VIII, 112
Mutiny, Incitement to   VIII, 110
Mutiny of No. 4 Battery   I, 20
Nanaimo   I, 15, 18;   II, 25, 27;   VI, 86
Narrows North Fort   V, 62, 63, 64, 84;   VII, 96, 98;   VIII, 105-109, 111
National Resources Mobilization Act   VIII, 108

H.M.S. Newcastle   III, 50;   VI, 86
Newington, The   VI, 86
News Advertiser Newspaper   II, 24, 25, 27, 29
Newton, Lancelot   I, 14
New Westminster   I, 12 and PASSIM;   II, 22, 24, 26;   III, 52;   IV, 55
New Westminster Municipal Council   I, 13
New Westminster Volunteer Rifles   I, 13, 15, 17, 21;   II, 24
New Yorker of Yorke Island   VI, 92
9.2-inch Coastal Guns   V, 64
H.M.C.S. Niobe   III, 32
Northwest Rebellion of 1885   I, 18
No. 1 Battery, B.C.B.G.A.   I, 19;   II, 24
No. 4 Battery, B.C.B.G.A.   I, 19, 20
No. 5 Battery, B.C.B.G.A.   II, 25
No. 6 Battery, B.C.B.G.A.   II, 27
Nurnburg, The   III, 31, 50, 53
Occupations of Militiamen   II, 29
Odlum, Victor W.   IV, 58
One-Inch Aiming Rifle   VII, 95;   VIII, 105
102nd Coast Regiment (Reserve), R.C.A.   VIII, 111
104th New Westminster Regiment   II, 30
Osborne, J.E.E.   VIII, 108
Oswell, E.H.   VIII, 105
Otter, Sir William   IV, 54
Ovens, Thomas   I, 20, 21
Parades   II, 25   See also Dominion Day Celebrations
Paterson, J.V.   III, 49
Pearl Harbour   VI, 92;   VIII, 106
Peele, Adolphus   I, 21
Pender, Daniel   II, 22
Peroune, G.P.   III, 52
Perry, R.T.   IV, 55
Personnel in Vancouver Defences   VII, 96;   VIII, 104, 106-108
Piercey, J.E.   VI, 89, 92
Pittendreigh, George   I, 16, 18, 19
H.M.S. Plumper   II, 22
Point Atkinson   II, 24;   V, 63, 64;   VII, 96, 98;   VIII, 106-107
Point Ellice Bridge Disaster   II, 28
Point Grey   II, 22;   III, 31, 51, 52;   IV, 59;   V, 61, 83;   VII, 98;   VIII, 104-108, 110-112
Point Grey Fort   V, 61-82, 83;   VII, 99   VIII, 104-108, 110-112
Port Moody   II, 22
Port War Signal Station   V, 64;   VII, 98
Port Wartime Security Regulations   VII, 98
Powlett, Capt.   VI, 86
Prince Robert, The   VI, 90
Prior, Edward Gawlor   I, 19, 20;   II, 25, 28, 29
Prohibition of Liquor   IV, 56, 57
Prospect Point   V, 62
Pumphrey, E.J.   III, 52

Queen Maude, The   VII, 98
Queensborough   I, 12
Radar (Radio/Direction/Finding)   VII, 98
H.M.C.S. Rainbow   III, 32, 50
Ramsay, R.M.   VI, 91
Recruiting   II, 25
Remains of Vancouver Defences in 1977   VIII, 111, 112
Rendezvous, The   VI, 92
Reunion Suppers   II, 30
Rhodes, G.   VIII, 106
Richards, George H.   II, 22;   VI, 85
Rogers, Mrs. B.T.   IV, 58
Robert Dunsmuir, The   II, 27
Robertson-Ross, Patrick   I, 15
Rosebrugh, C.K.   VII, 95;   VIII, 107
Royal Canadian Air Force   V, 63, 64
Royal Canadian Army Medical Corps   II, 30;   VI, 89, 90;   VIII, 108
Royal Canadian Army Service Corps   II, 30;   VI, 90
Royal Canadian Engineers   II, 30;   V, 61;   VI, 90;   VIII, 107
Royal Canadian Navy   III, 32;   V, 62, 63;   VI, 90;   VII, 96
Royal Canadian Ordnance Corps   V, 84
Royal Engineers   I, 12, 14
Royal Navy   I, 16;   II, 24, 28;   III, 49   IV, 58
Russia   I, 16, 17;   II, 24;   III, 53
Salmon River Logging Company   VI, 88
Salvation Army   VII, 100
Sarcee Camp   IV, 56, 57
Scheme of Defence for B.C.   V, 62, 63
Scott, John F.   I, 15, 16
Sea Island Airport   VIII, 106
Seattle   II, 29
Seattle Construction and Dry Dock Company   III, 49
Second Battalion, 5th Regiment, C.A.   I, 20;   II, 28, 29;
Selbie, H.W.   VIII, 107
Selby-Smyth, Sir Edward   I, 16
Semple, Capt.   VII, 100
Setterfield, A.C.   VIII, 105, 106
17th (North B.C.) Coast Regiment, R.C.A.   VIII, 107
Seymour Artillery Company or Seymour Battery   I, 14, 15, 16, 17;   II, 25;
Seymour Narrows   III, 51;   VI, 86
Sham Battles   II, 28, 30
Sharp, H.T.   II, 26
Shilo (Manitoba)   IV, 59
Singapore   VII, 101
Sino-Japanese War   V, 82
Siwash Point Battery   III, 51;
Siwash Rock   VIII, 111
6-Inch Coastal Guns   IV, 59;   V, 61, 63, 64;   VI, 92;
6-Pounder Duplex Guns   IV, 59;   VIII, 106

6-Pounder Hotchkiss Guns VI, 88, 91;
   VII, 98;
Sixth Battalion (Duke of Connaught's Own)
   Rifles I, 20; II, 29-30
6th Light Anti-Aircraft Regiment, R.C.A.
   VI, 92
60-Pounder Field Guns III, 51; IV, 57;
68th Battery, C.F.A. IV, 55, 60
68th Overseas Depot Battery III, 52
64-Pounder Guns at Vancouver II, 27, 30;
Smallwood, C.P.O. VI, 87
Smith, Harry V, 82
Smith, John I, 14
Smyth, Connie VI, 92
Spanish-American War II, 29
Spanish Banks VII, 98
Spanish Civil War V, 82
Stacey, Charles P. VIII, 112
Stanley Park II, 22; III, 51, 52;
   IV, 55, 60; V, 61, 63, 64, 83;
   VII, 98, 101;
   VII, 104, 105, 111
Stephens, James I, 21
Stevens, H.H. III, 52
Steveston V, 63, 64, 84; VII, 96, 99;
   VIII, 106, 107
Stewart, A.M. III, 52
Stewart, J.C. IV, 59; V, 61
Stewart, J.M. III, 52
Stopping or Heave-To Rounds VI, 88;
   VII, 98-100; VIII, 105
Strange, T. Bland I, 18
Stursberg, Peter VII, 95
Submarines IV, 59, 60; VII, 101;
   VIII, 105, 108
Submarines CC1 and CC2 III, 49
Supermarine Stranraer V, 64
Sydney (Australia) VII, 96
Thackray, W.C. VIII, 105 (N.B. Quotation has
   "Thackery" but this is an error)
3rd Searchlight Battery, 1st Searchlight Regi-
   ment, R.C.A. VI, 90; VII, 96
13 Pounder Anti-Aircraft Guns V, 82
31st Battery, C.F.A. IV, 55, 57
31st Heavy Battery, R.C.A. V, 61; VII, 96;
   VIII, 104, 106
Thompson River I, 12
3-Pounder Sub-Calibre Tubes VII, 94
3.7-Inch Heavy Anti-Aircraft Guns V, 83;
   VIII, 107
Torpedo Boats III, 50; IV, 59
Townley, C.R. I, 20
Townley, Thomas Owen I, 19;
   II, 24, 25, 28
Townsley, W.A. IV, 58
Train, George Francis I, 13
Treatt, B.D.C. IV, 59; V, 82; VI 86, 92
Triggs, Gnr. VII, 98
Tsingtao III, 31
Turner, John II, 26

Tweedsmuir, Lord V, 84
12-Pounder, Quick-Firing Guns IV, 59;
   V, 63, 64, 82;
24th Anti-Tank Battery, R.C.A. VII, 102
25-Pounder Gun/Howitzer VIII, 106
28th Anti-Aircraft Regiment, R.C.A. V, 83;
   VIII, 105, 111
2-Pounder, Naval Anti-Aircraft Gun VII, 100;
   VIII, 105, 106;
Uniforms I, 17; II, 29; IV, 59; VI, 87;
   VII, 101, 102
United Service Centre VIII, 109
United States I, 12, 13; II, 22, 24, 29;
   III, 49, 50; IV, 59; VII, 94, 101, 103
United States Navy IV, 58
University Endowment Lands II, 22
University of British Columbia V, 83;
   VIII, 111, 112
Vancouver I, 15, 18; II, 22 and **PASSIM**
Vancouver as a Military Target V, 82
Vancouver Board of Trade III, 52; IV, 56
Vancouver Daily Province Newspaper III, 32,
   50; IV, 58; VI, 86;
   VII, 94, 100
Vancouver Defences Recommended in 1937
   IV, 59
Vancouver Island I, 12, 13, 15; II, 22, 28;
   IV, 59; V, 82; VI, 86, 92
Vancouver Kinsmen IV, 58
Vancouver Parks Board VIII, 111
Vancouver Sun Newspaper VII, 100
Vancouver Town Planning Commission IV, 59
Vancouver Volunteer Reserve or Home Guard
   III, 51, 52
Venereal Diseases VIII, 108, 110
Veterans Guard VI, 90
Vianen, W.H. I, 21
Victoria, B.C. I, 15-17, 18-20; II, 24, 25, 28;
   III, 49; IV, 55
Victoria Day Celebrations I, 17, 18, 20, 21;
   II, 28
Victoria - Esquimalt Defences III, 32; V, 64;
   VII, 94; VIII, 111
Vladivostok II, 24
Von Spee, Count Maximilian III, 31, 50, 53;
   VI, 86
Wadsley VIII, 106
War Diaries of Coastal Forts VIII, 104-108
H.M.C.S. **West Coast** VI, 88
Whitehead, F.C. VIII, 106
Wiesenborn, J.R. I, 16
Woodward, W.C. IV, 58; VIII, 108
Worsnop, Charles Arthur II, 25, 28, 29;
   III, 52
Y.M.C.A. VI, 92
York, The VI, 88
Yorke Island IV, 59, 60; V, 61, 63, 64;
   VI, 85 and **PASSIM**; VII, 102
   VIII, 104, 108, 111
"Zombies" VIII, 110

UA
601
B7
M66

OCT 9 1979